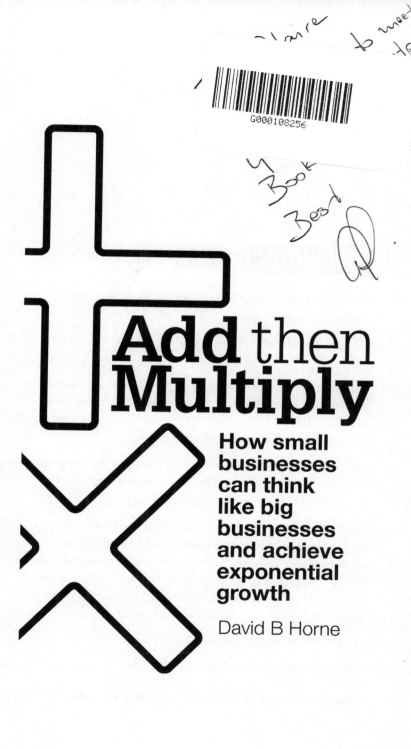

Add then Multiply

How small businesses can think like big businesses and achieve exponential growth

David B Horne

RETHINK PRESS

First published in Great Britain in 2019 by Rethink Press
(www.rethinkpress.com)

© Copyright David B Horne

Cover artwork by David Carroll & Co

Author photograph by Clark Smith-Stanley

Printed and bound by CPI Group (UK) Ltd, Croydon, CR0 4YY

Praise

'This book piqued my interest when it promised insights on how to fund, acquire, consolidate and exit businesses, which are areas I've had no experience in. David takes you through the numbers and the psychology of doing major business deals with visceral stories and at times it felt like I was getting the inside story from Richard Branson's special ops team. Growing a business 10x and more in three years is something few of us have a playbook for, which puts this one firmly in the category of recommended reading for all entrepreneurs.'
— Mark Robinson, Founder, Rocksteady Music School

'Wherever your business is in its lifecycle, making decisions about resources as well as how the business evolution fits in with your personal goals and values is key. *Add Then Multiply* invites you to revisit your vision as you go on a journey of business and personal growth. Through a series of case studies and real-life examples, David B Horne demystifies some of the common investment terms, helping you understand which would be best for you in terms of making major decisions about investment partners. Whether you are a business owner looking for exponential growth, an investment partner or someone working in a fast-growing business, *Add Then Multiply* is a handy reference that highlights both the hard and soft issues you need to be aware of.'
— Rupa Datta, Founder, Portfolio People

'I met David in the year 2000, and since then we have worked together in several different businesses – as colleagues, clients and advisors to each other. He has a unique combination of finance skills and real understanding of people, something I've not seen in any other finance person I've met. His book *Add Then Multiply* applies his background in international listed companies with great intelligence and success. This book gives readers business stories that are packed full of experience, and David presents his FACE methodology – Fund, Acquire, Consolidate, Exit – in a way that is clear and understandable. If you're an entrepreneur interested in serious growth, read this book.'

    — Martin Porter, Co-Founder, The Centre International, and Executive Chair, Brussels at the Cambridge Institute for Sustainability Leadership

'Today, more than ever, we live in a time where entrepreneurship is the engine room that drives the economy. New businesses are starting in every sector imaginable. Whilst many of them are focused on growing their business organically, in his book *Add Then Multiply*, David B Horne is changing the rules on this and bringing you his experience of raising funds and growing businesses through the acquisition and consolidation of other companies. His FACE methodology tells how to scale up much faster than many would have thought possible. With his warm conversational style, backed up

with plenty of detail from real businesses that have done this before, David has written a book that is both engaging and informative. Every entrepreneur who is serious about growth could take something from this book, if only to challenge their own assumptions.'
— Mary Monfries, Partner and Private Client Leader, PricewaterhouseCoopers LLP

'I have known David for more than 15 years and worked with him on several of the deals he talks about in this book, which brings the world of high finance to life in a way that every successful entrepreneur should understand. This is not something that's reserved for big corporates. In addition to the technical aspects of his FACE methodology, David tells stories based on his experience of the deals and the people involved. It is an engaging and entertaining read for any entrepreneur who wants to really grow their business and do it quickly. I highly recommend this book.'
— Jamie Matheson, Executive Chairman (retired), Brewin Dolphin Holdings PLC

'I worked with David on several fundraising projects and a substantial global acquisition. His book *Add Then Multiply* and his FACE methodology are a refreshing take on fundraising, acquisitions, consolidation and exits, and he has a clear focus on bringing awareness and understanding of this to the world of entrepreneurship. Packed full of real stories from deals that David has done, this book is a must-read for every entrepreneur who wants to know more about rapid growth using a buy-and-build strategy and ultimately exiting their business.'

— Delphine Currie, Partner, global law firm

'David B Horne knows how to do deals. We have worked together on many, both large and small, since 2003. In this book, David takes the reader on a journey through each step of his FACE methodology, with clear and very readable stories of fundraising, acquisitions, consolidation and exits. Not only does it cover the technical aspects of the methodology, this book also covers the mindset needed to build a business very quickly following these steps. Entrepreneurs who are serious about growing their business can use this book as a guide on the path of exponential growth.'

— Ronald Paterson, Partner, Eversheds
    Sutherland (International) LLP

Contents

For Kate, Vicky and Madsie:
'You Are the Everything'*

Foreword

'Fund, acquire, consolidate, exit'. In four words, I knew David B Horne had a lot of value to share with the entrepreneur community.

David jumped on to my radar during a pitching competition we were running at Dent Global. He was a participant on our Key Person of Influence Accelerator, but it wasn't until the last event that I really clocked him.

He gave an exceptional pitch. David shared how his background working at PricewaterhouseCoopers (PwC), his experience as a CFO in two public companies raising over £100,000,000 of funding and doing dozens of deals had given him unique insights. All of this experience had culminated in a strategy that could accelerate the success of entrepreneurial companies. A strategy that I knew most entrepreneurs were not even aware of, let alone using.

The strategy involves raising funding and achieving a benchmark valuation, then acquiring new businesses that are a good strategic fit. An acquisition brings instant uplift, but it also brings instant complexity challenges that need to be consolidated: the third step. Finally, after a combination of organic growth and acquired businesses, the opportunity to exit the business is present.

Fund, acquire, consolidate, exit.

I had seen this strategy work for one of my mentors who had made millions each time he applied it. I had not seen someone break it down as elegantly and simply as David has, so that any entrepreneur can implement it.

As a result of David's pitch, I set up a meeting with him and appointed him as CFO of Dent Global (a part-time role where we had him for two to four days a month). Rapidly, we completed several deals that involved achieving a higher valuation for Dent Global and acquiring complementary businesses. We also identified several opportunities to take strategic stakes in businesses we could see promise in.

I've not completed the final step – exit – because Dent is still 'my baby'. I love the business far too much to see it pass to anyone else just yet and I still see many years of growth and fun ahead. But if I did want to exit, I'd now be in a strong position to do so as a result of David's assistance and his clear strategy.

Dent Global has worked closely with over 3,000 companies in the UK, Australia, Singapore and the USA. We see behind the scenes how entrepreneurs are running and growing their businesses. One thing is certain, the vast majority of entrepreneurs are not aware of or implementing a strategy of growth through acquisition.

It amazes me that in the entrepreneurial community, there's a strong conversation about innovation, marketing or digital transformation, but you rarely hear about buying a business that is a strategic fit. If you peel back the layers on most big success stories in business, they almost always include an acquisition or two. Many 'dragons' or 'sharks' grew their businesses through acquisitions. Most big-name entrepreneurial success involves funding, acquiring, consolidating and exiting, even more so than growing organically.

Your own entrepreneurial success story will benefit greatly from the strategy contained in this book. When you start funding your ideas, you'll be able to take action much faster. When you acquire complementary businesses, you'll take strategic leaps forward. When you consolidate, you'll have a seamless business that runs smoothly despite its accelerated growth. When you exit, you'll have capital and time available to move into a new adventure.

David is the perfect person to take you on this journey. Beyond his deep experience, he is the type of business leader you'd want to have on your team. In the movies, people who do lots of big deals are a bit crass, a bit brash and a bit loose with the truth. David is the opposite of all those things – he's genuine, he's thoughtful and he's honest. All of this comes across in the book and reassures you that if you've built a growing business based on good principles, you'll be able to adopt his strategy without compromising your integrity.

Fund, acquire, consolidate, exit. It is an advanced strategy for achieving accelerated growth. It might well be the strategy that unleashes your full potential as an entrepreneur and helps you achieve your vision of success.

Daniel Priestley
Co-founder and CEO of Dent Global,
and best-selling author of *Key Person of Influence*,
Entrepreneur Revolution, Oversubscribed and *24 Assets*

Introduction

Imagine you could grow your business 10× or more in just three years. As entrepreneurs, we are all about growth, but that kind of growth is out of the ordinary. For many established businesses, organic growth of 20–25% a year represents a stretching objective, and as you go through certain stages as a business, you hit pain points. Imagine you didn't have to do that. Imagine there was another way.

There is. I've done it.

You'll need to change the rules of the game and play it with a different mindset. In this book you will learn from my real-life experiences how you can transform your business and achieve 10× growth and more in a much shorter period of time than you may have thought possible. To paraphrase Liam Neeson's character Bryan Mills in the film *Taken*: I have a unique set of skills that I've developed over a long career. Unlike Mr Neeson's character, though, my skills make me useful to you, rather than a nightmare!

In recent years, entrepreneurship has taken off. It has never been easier to launch a business, and with consumers using the internet around the world, running a global business is no longer restricted to large multi-national corporations. Everyone has the potential to do it.

Government statistics show that in 2018, there were 5,668,000 businesses in the UK. Of those, 5,415,000 had fewer than ten employees (micro-businesses), leaving 210,000 small businesses (employing between ten and forty-nine people), 35,000 medium businesses (employing 50–249 people) and 8,000 large businesses (employing more than 250 people). This book is targeted at the owners of the 245,000 small and medium enterprises (SMEs) in the UK, and to their counterparts in countries around the world.

Organic growth is hard work. Most businesses start that way, and it is the natural way for them to do so: identify a problem that the market has, create a solution that solves the problem, find the customer and sell them your solution. It's a classic model that works, but it's hard work and it takes a long time.

Once you reach, say, £1 million in sales and you carry on growing at 20–25% per annum, it will take you three or four years to double your sales to £2 million. To grow your business tenfold at those organic rates would take eleven to thirteen years. Growing at 20–25% consistently is not easy. Slow growth down to 10% and it'll take you eight years to double and twenty-five years to multiply your sales by ten. Long, hard years of slogging it out, and no doubt in that period of time there will be ups and downs associated with economic cycles. It could take longer.

What if there was a better way? A way that you could scale your business, take out competitors and reach more customers with more products and services in more locations? A way that would get you to the big negotiating tables in your industry that you'd previously thought were unattainable? A way that you could do this fast? By changing the rules of the game and playing it with a different mindset, you can achieve that kind of growth.

Growing 10× and more in three years is doable. I've done it before and am going to share how I did it with you in this book. Taking everything I have learned over more than thirty years in business, I have developed a methodology called FACE, which stands for:

- Fund

- Acquire

- Consolidate

- Exit

This is something that large companies and multi-national corporations use to grow. I know, because it's what I used to do when I worked for global corporates and companies listed on the stock exchange early in my career. Now I no longer work for listed companies or multi-national corporations; since 2010, I have worked exclusively with entrepreneurs and founders of businesses. It's much more fun – they get things done faster and there's way less politics. Several of my clients are global businesses with customers and operations in more than their home country.

After many years of learning on the job, figuring things out and investing in my own personal development, I have adapted the big-company approach and developed my FACE methodology to use with SME businesses. It is a methodology that allows the owners of businesses to scale quickly and to achieve their dreams.

Come with me on a journey that changes the rules and unlocks exponential growth: a journey that explains why I have chosen to write this book. It's not a book for everyone. It's not even for all the owners of the 245,000 SMEs in the UK or their counterparts around the world. It's for the select few who are open to playing by a new set of rules.

Are you one of the select few?

This book is structured in two parts, plus a conclusion and appendices:

- Part I – Getting Ready

- Part II – The FACE Methodology

- Conclusion – It's Time To FACE Your Future

- The appendices deal in more detail with some technical matters that are referred to in the book, but not everyone wants the technical details

I'll close this introduction with one of my favourite quotes:

'This is the true joy in life, the being used for a purpose recognized by yourself as a mighty one; the being thoroughly worn out before you are thrown on the scrap heap; the being a force of Nature instead of a feverish selfish little clod of ailments and grievances complaining that the world will not devote itself to making you happy.

'I am of the opinion that my life belongs to the community, and as long as I live, it is my privilege to do for it whatever I can. I want

to be thoroughly used up when I die, for the harder I work, the more I live. Life is no "brief candle" to me. It is a sort of splendid torch which I have got hold of for a moment, and I want to make it burn as brightly as possible before handing it on to the future generations.'
— George Bernard Shaw

For now, I ask you to pick up your splendid torch and let me show you how to make it burn as brightly as possible.

PART ONE
GETTING READY

1
Your Business

'To begin with the end in mind means to start with a clear understanding of your destination. It means to know where you're going so that you better understand where you are now and so that the steps you take are always in the right direction.'
— Stephen R Covey

Important first steps

Before we move on to discuss how you can implement the FACE methodology, there are a couple of things you need to be crystal clear about, both of which involve some serious looking within. In this chapter we will focus our attention on your business, and in the next chapter we'll explore what's going on in your head. Please don't skip this section – these are both important, because if you are to achieve the kind of growth we are talking about, your business and your head need to be in the right place. I've seen many businesses grow quickly without the owner ensuring the basics were in place, and it often ended badly. Being sure that you and your business are ready is critical to ensuring success.

We will be looking at four areas in this chapter – values and culture, people, brand, and systems and processes – in the context of why they are important before you execute the FACE methodology.

Company values and culture

Values are at the very heart of your business, one of the guiding principles that inform both big strategic decisions and day-to-day activities. You need to use them in the recruitment and retention of staff, because they have such an impact on the way everyone behaves. They drive the culture of your business.

As such, it is critical that you document your values and share them with your staff, showing as the leader of the business that you live those values. It doesn't need to be a long, complicated document. In fact, broadly speaking, the shorter the better.

One of my favourite examples of a statement of values comes from the global healthcare business, Johnson &

Johnson. In 1943 Robert Wood Johnson, a member of the founding family, crafted a document called 'Our Credo'. It opens with the following statement: 'We believe our first responsibility is to the patients, doctors and nurses, to mothers and fathers and all others who use our products and services.' The credo goes on to say the company also has responsibility, in descending order, to its employees; to the communities where they live and work, and to the global community; and to its shareholders.

The credo played a huge part in decision-making during the Tylenol crisis of 1982, when seven people in Chicago died because someone had tampered with Tylenol bottles and replaced the pain-killing medicine with poison. As soon as the company discovered this, the board of directors took no time at all in deciding to put out advertisements across the United States telling people not to take Tylenol. They asked retailers to remove the product from the shelves of their stores and instructed their supply chain to destroy the entire stock of Tylenol. No matter the cost, their first responsibility was clear.

Nearly forty years later, the reaction by Johnson & Johnson is still considered a masterclass in successful crisis management. The values were clear and guided everyone's behaviour.

Your business may not have the size and scope of a global company like Johnson & Johnson, and hopefully people will not die if one of your products proves to be faulty or is tampered with. Nonetheless, if you are going to be growing by acquisition and bringing other companies with their own values and culture into your business, it is imperative that you have one set of values and culture for the entire organisation. This is a big issue that we will deal with further in Part II. For now, I urge you to ensure that you and your entire team have clarity about what your values are, and that you live them every day. Without clarity over your values today and the culture that they drive, you will have an enormous challenge when you acquire and consolidate other businesses into your own.

People

Many entrepreneurs display super-human characteristics in terms of stamina, determination and drive. It is fully accepted that nobody will ever care as much about your business as you do, but make no mistake. Implementing the FACE methodology is not something you can do on your own. You need a team of skilled and experienced people to play their part – both in running the existing business and in dealing with the fundraising, acquisitions and consolidation. The exit may come a little later down the line, and the team will play their part then too.

Every business is different and unique, and yet in so many ways, every business is also the same. They all find and win customers. They deliver the product or service to customers. They invoice customers and collect money. They pay staff and suppliers. Hopefully at the end there is money left to reinvest in the business and to pay the owners. At its simplest level, that means every business has three core departments reporting to the chief executive:

- Sales and marketing, whose job it is to find and win customers

- Operations, whose job it is to deliver the product or service to customers and ensure they are happy

- Finance, whose job it is to handle everything to do with money

In the early stages of a company, the founder will often fulfil one or more of those roles, but as the company grows and becomes more complex, they become too big for one person. To address these challenges, the founder must hire specialist talent. Each of these teams will expand to support the business as it grows and enable it to grow further, but for the purposes of this discussion, we'll just focus on the three departments as whole entities.

Before implementing the FACE methodology, you must have strong leaders of those three core departments in place. They will be entrusted with much of the day-to-day business activities while your attention may be elsewhere: meeting with potential investors, advisors and possible acquisition candidates, and negotiating the deal, which can become an all-consuming activity for you.

At various stages of implementation of the FACE methodology, you will also need to draw on your senior team to pitch in and play their part with the additional workload that is heading their way. The sales and marketing leader and the operations leader will both be involved in the due diligence stage of acquisitions and will be heavily involved in consolidating the newly acquired company's people, products and services, systems and processes into your company. The finance leader will likely be involved in every stage of the FACE methodology.

Brand

This is the core of the business you have built. It's the soft stuff; the intangible stuff; that which truly sets you apart from the competition. It doesn't matter if your business operates in a highly commoditised industry or one that is niche, with few competitors. The brand is what makes your business unique. The brand is what people know, like and trust.

It's so much more than just your company name or logo. It's deeply ingrained in the philosophy and ethos behind your business: how your staff answer the phone or communicate via email; how they interact with customers and suppliers; even how they interact with competitors.

Marketers often talk about how a brand has personality and describe brands as if they were people, complete with their own blend of emotional, rational and sensual attributes. The emotional side is linked to psychology and how customers feel when they use your brand. What is appealing about it? What makes customers feel good? The rational side is all about how your product or service performs, and whether it solves the customer's problems. The sensual side is the physical attributes that are linked to the five senses. How does it look? How does it sound? Smell? Taste? Feel?

Every entrepreneur I have met has worked hard to establish their brand, and the biggest challenge to that comes when the business grows – when you bring in new members of staff, or entire companies once you start making acquisitions. The most important thing about the brand is that it must be consistent. It is likely that you will be the brand guardian, but you need to delegate the day-to-day aspects of that guardianship to a member of your team.

Protecting the brand is critically important, so you must ensure that you have the right protections in place over your brand and any associated intellectual property (IP). If you haven't done so already, seek out an IP lawyer and have a chat. You need to have established and documented brand guidelines, which everyone within the company has access to and follows. For a few thousand pounds you can put in place protections that prevent others from stealing that which you have worked so hard to develop.

Finally, keep an open mind as you implement the FACE methodology. You may have the opportunity to acquire other businesses whose brands you admire. You may find a part of your business would benefit from ditching its brand entirely in favour of another one that has better or more powerful recognition in your industry. You'll read about a couple of examples of this later in the book.

Systems and processes

Systems and processes, especially processes, go well beyond just thinking about information technology, programmes and applications. This is all about the everyday stuff that happens in your business. It's linked to your brand, because it is what your customers and suppliers experience each time they interact with your company. It's linked to your people, because it drives the work they do each day. It's linked to your values, because they are what guides your company.

Some companies choose to document their systems and processes at a high level, covering the inputs, a brief description of the process and the outputs it creates. Other companies go into great detail on a step-by-step basis of what happens for everything that goes on in the company. A few don't document any processes at all, and that's a big risk.

The level of detail behind the systems and processes will vary depending on the nature of the business and the people who are driving it. Before you implement the FACE methodology, I strongly recommend that you sit down with your top team and ensure you have an agreed level of documentation over at least these processes:

- Sales and marketing – identifying and targeting prospective customers; progressing them through the sales funnel; closing the deal; the handover to operations

- Operations – setting up and managing customers; purchasing and stock control; product or service delivery; quality control; customer service

- Finance – raising and collecting sales invoices; processing and paying purchase invoices; payroll and employee expenses; financial reporting; cash flow

- Human resources – hiring, retaining and firing people

Chapter wrap

This is a short chapter which has dealt with the topics at a high level, its objective being to ensure you think about and action each of the areas it has covered so that you are ready to implement the FACE methodology. I'm not an expert in those areas, but I know from many years' experience that they need to be in place for you to succeed as you embark on a journey of exponential growth. They are like the foundations of a building that you will be constructing later.

In this chapter, we've covered:

- Being crystal clear about your values and culture, and ensuring these are understood throughout your company

- Making sure you have the right people in place to take your business forward as it expands

- Ensuring your brand and IP are clearly set out and appropriately protected

- Having the systems and processes documented that allow your company to run smoothly and to take on more as you integrate newly acquired companies into your business

More than anything else, the thing I want you to take away from this chapter is the fact that you need a team of strong, experienced people leading the core functions of your business. You cannot implement the FACE methodology alone.

2
Your Head

'Thought is the vehicle that will take you to the secret
knowledge that lies at the root of all human experience... It
is fluid and can be molded to suit the day.'
— Sydney Banks

What I'm going to share with you in this chapter
may well need a change in your mindset. It's
different and challenges conventional thinking. The
thing is, it works. So stick with me.

Challenging conventional thinking

The pace of change in today's world is so fast that you
need to think differently if you want to get ahead. It's
the only way.

You can of course choose not to change. You can slog it out in your industry, fighting battles with the same competitors, undercutting them to win the next job, but it's a race to the bottom. It's sad, really. In my years in business I've come across so many entrepreneurs who started out with a dream, and then reality bit them. Hard. I've seen founders who had great vision, but ten years on their business still hasn't broken through seven-figures in sales. They barely take a holiday, and when they do they're always on the phone or the laptop back to the office. It takes a huge toll on their family. Some are still struggling to get by on average earnings. In the UK, that's just £27K per annum, and you can't live a great life on that. Their dream is dead, and they feel trapped.

Instead of growing, they try to cut back to save money: 'Let's spend less on marketing. We don't need to update our website, it's only five years old. It's hard to find skilled workers and they're so expensive. Let's get cheap ones instead.' It works, for a while, but it makes it impossible to grow a business.

It's a mindset thing. If all you think about is cutting back and saving money, you'll never break out of that rut. It's pervasive. Your staff and culture soon reflect it. The thing is, *everything* we experience in life is dependent upon our thinking in the moment. The world outside us is not responsible for our experience and how we feel about it; the world outside us merely gives us input through our five senses. Only we are able to decide how we feel, and our thinking affects that. Most times it doesn't seem that way, but that really is how it works.

This isn't just some new-age hippy thing. There's a wonderful quote from Henry Ford, perhaps the most successful entrepreneur of his time, who said over a hundred years ago: 'Whether you think you can, or you think you can't – you're right.' More than seventy years ago, Viktor Frankl was a Jewish prisoner of the Nazis in World War II. All of his family were killed in concentration camps, but he survived and thrived (as much as one can under such inhumane conditions). Frankl discovered that, no matter what his captors did to him, he retained the final freedom: to choose how to react to what was happening to him. His thinking led to him being described as the freest man in those death camps.

What does all this mindset stuff have to do with entrepreneurship and growing your business? Everything, really. Changing your mindset is changing the rules to unlock exponential growth. It's about having an open mind and the willingness to challenge what many people perceive as conventional wisdom, or indeed common sense.

When you implement the FACE methodology, it'll be like riding a rollercoaster. There will be new challenges, new opportunities and new emotional responses. There will be wins. There will be setbacks.

It's inevitable. You are creating a new future for yourself and your company. You need to have clarity over where you are now and where you want to go, and you need an open mind to move forward.

Reconnecting with your vision

Let's take a little time to go back to the vision you had when you started your business. When he launched Microsoft, Bill Gates famously said that he had the vision of a personal computer on every desk and in every home. Steve Jobs, before he was fired by the Apple board, secured the services of John Sculley as the new CEO by challenging him with the question, 'Do you want to sell sugar water for the rest of your life, or do you want to come with me and change the world?'

I'd like you to take a moment now and think back to the day you launched your business. Most business owners I meet had a vision of something they wanted to achieve. Something that drove them to take the plunge into the world of entrepreneurship. Like Bill Gates or Steve Jobs, they saw how they wanted to change the world, or at least their part of the world. Think back and remember how that felt. When you implement the FACE methodology, you'll have the opportunity to turbocharge the achievement of your vision.

Your most valuable currency

One of the most challenging discussions I have with entrepreneurs relates to their reluctance to 'give away equity'. It's an expression that bugs me, because it puts an immediate limit on their ability to achieve exponential growth. This is a mindset thing. Something tells entrepreneurs that they must be in complete control of their business, and that means they must be in complete control of the equity. That doesn't have to be the case.

Let me set the record straight here: equity should never be given away. Equity is the entrepreneur's most valuable currency. By all means exchange it for something of equal or greater value, but *never* give it away.

Please take time to make sure you have a clear understanding of this concept. For some it comes easily. For others it's really hard to grasp because it flies in the face of being the master or mistress of your own destiny. It may require a complete 180 degree turn in the way you think about your business. Your brain can handle that. Let me restate two sentences from the previous paragraph, because this is fundamental to everything else we are going to talk about: 'equity is the entrepreneur's most valuable currency. By all means exchange it for something of equal or greater value, but *never* give it away.'

It's a similar thing when people talk about their stake being diluted when a company issues more shares. If they don't want their percentage holding to reduce, then they can follow their investment and buy more shares when they are issued. Paradoxically, if the value of the shares has gone up, the value of their holding has too, even if their percentage stake declines. There's an old saying that goes along the lines of 'Would you rather own 100% of a local car dealership or 1% of General Motors?' General Motors was at a time in the 20th century one of the biggest, most respected companies on the planet. Perhaps the updated version would be 'Would you rather own 100% of a local computer company or 1% of Apple?' – I'm sure you get the gist.

To gain the most from the FACE methodology – which I will share with you in detail in Part II of the book – you must be comfortable with the fact that other people may have an ownership stake and a say about what goes on in your company. That's a mindset thing, and that's why I've been talking about the human mind in this chapter. Indeed, if you follow the FACE methodology fully, you may end up owning less than 50% of your company. You may not have control, but the value of your holding could be exponentially more than it is today.

For some entrepreneurs, not being in complete control is not OK. I've met many who are strongly of the view that they must own and control everything. If that's you, then I suggest you put this book down. You've come to the wrong place. It's not that there's anything wrong with wanting to own and control everything, but it's not what this book is about.

OK, you're still with me? That's great. Let's explore this in a little more depth.

Let's say that your company is worth £3 million and you want to raise £2 million in funding (we'll get into the details later, just go with me on this for now). After the investor's money is put in, the company is now worth £5 million (the £3 million value plus the £2 million cash). There's a subtle shift in wording here. Did you notice it?

The company now has a value of £5 million. You own 60% of it, which is the £3 million the company was worth before you raised the money. The investor (for simplicity's sake let's assume it is one investor) owns 40% of it, which is the £2 million that she paid in, in return for equity. You didn't give it away, did you? You sold it. You're still the larger shareholder and on a day-to-day basis you're likely to call the shots. You're probably the founder as well, and that will never change. Steve Jobs was always the founder of Apple, even when he got fired by the board and left the company.

The subtle shift is the change from 'your company' to 'the company'. It's a really important thing for you to grasp and understand. There is now a co-owner of the company. It's likely that she will sit on the board of directors and have a say in the strategic decisions that affect the business. After all, she has made the investment and wants to see that it is being used wisely and in accordance with the plans that you agreed between you when she invested.

Let's stick with the company that's now worth £5 million and take another example. Let's talk about stock options. These are often used to attract and retain key employees. You grant an option to a key member of staff, say a new chief technology officer (CTO) for a growing tech business, that gives them the right (but not the obligation) to buy shares in the company at a date in the future, based on a price you set up front in the option agreement. If the CTO chooses to exercise the option, then he will pay the agreed price in return for shares in the company. If he doesn't exercise the option, then it will lapse and nothing happens.

Let's say he does exercise the option, which allows him to buy 5% of the equity in the company. In this case, you and your investor each get diluted by 5%. So now the ownership is as follows:

- You own 57% (95% of the 60% you held previously)

- The investor owns 38% (95% of the 40% she held previously)

- The CTO owns 5%

Did you 'give away' any equity here? No, you sold equity in the form of an option to attract and retain the services of a CTO who will be critical to the future growth of the company, and he paid money into the company in exchange for the shares. You exchanged equity for something of equal or greater value.

We'll fast forward a few years and assume the company is now worth £10 million thanks to the great strategy that you executed, funded by the investor and developed by the CTO. Your stake in the business is now worth £5.7 million. The investor's stake is now worth £3.8 million and the CTO's stake is worth £500,000. You and the investor have nearly doubled your money. You don't own 100% of the company and you don't control everything. But your shares in the company have increased in value from £3 million to £5.7 million. Give away equity? I don't think so. You've made smart decisions that have increased your net worth by 90%. The investor and the CTO have also benefited, so it's win-win-win.

The alternative of course is to stick with organic growth. If you want to spend ten or more years to achieve what can be done in three, that's your choice. I don't mind. But armed with your clear picture of how you can change the world, why would you want to wait so long? It's still hard work, but three years rather than ten or more is pretty appealing, don't you think? If you're not sure, I urge you to go back to the beginning of Part I and read it again.

If you're ready, then read on to learn how the FACE methodology was developed, followed by a case study of a business in which I helped grow revenues by 25× and profits by 11× in just three years. Now that's exponential growth.

Chapter wrap

In this chapter we've covered:

- Taking a new perspective on thought and mindset
- Reconnecting with the vision you had when you started your business
- The paradox that value can be gained by not having 100% control

More than anything else, the thing I want you to take away from this chapter is that equity is the entrepreneur's most valuable currency. Use it as such. Please get comfortable with this one.

3

Changing The Rules

'Everyone has his own specific vocation or mission in
life; everyone must carry out a concrete assignment that
demands fulfilment. Therein he cannot be replaced, nor can
his life be repeated, thus everyone's task is unique as is his
specific opportunity.'
— Viktor Frankl

OK, your business is in good shape and your head is
in the right place, so why listen to me and change
the rules? What's my story and how did the FACE
methodology evolve from that?

How I learned about changing the rules

I believe, as Viktor Frankl says, that each and every
one of us is on this planet for a reason. Many of us

never discover that reason, nor indeed are we even aware that there may be one.

There's an intertwining of business, money and travel experiences that dates back to the 1970s. I was born in Vancouver and grew up in a city called Victoria, on the west coast of Canada. In 1973, aged eleven, I got my first job as a newspaper boy, delivering the local morning paper, *The Daily Colonist*. The job had two main responsibilities: delivering newspapers each morning to a selection of about sixty or seventy homes in a particular area, and at the end of each month, ringing the doorbells and collecting cash from my customers. Once I had collected all the money , the area manager for the newspaper would come to my house and take the share that belonged to the newspaper. The rest was mine to keep. It was a good early lesson in business because it taught me in a hands-on way about delivering a product, keeping customers happy and dealing with money.

One day the area manager asked if I liked collecting money. It was my favourite part of the job. I loved the interaction with customers, getting to know them as people as opposed to just throwing a folded-up newspaper onto their front porch. I learned little things about them, like the old lady who had back troubles and found it hard to bend down and pick up her newspaper. She asked me to put it in her letterbox instead of throwing it onto the porch. Every month after that, she gave me a $5 tip.

I also loved to organise the money. Maybe it was a bit of obsessive compulsive disorder, but I used to make sure that all the banknotes were uncrumpled, unfolded and lined up with the Queen's head facing the same way. All the bills would be organised by denomination: $20, $10, $5, $2 and $1, something I still do with my cash today. I would organise any coins I'd collected and roll them up when quantities were right, taking them to the bank to exchange for notes. When the area manager came to collect the newspaper's share of the money, it was there ready for him, in nicely organised notes and as few coins as possible. Always the exact amount that the newspaper company was owed.

Then one day he asked if I would like to collect more money for the newspaper, as there were some people who were happy delivering the paper, but they didn't do a good job of the money side of things. In return, I earned a percentage of the money collected. This sounded like a great deal. I could collect money from customers at a much more sociable time (delivery of the newspaper had to be finished before 7am), interact with people, and handle the cash.

It was a no-brainer decision. I didn't think about it at the time, but it was a good decision by the area manager too. He had way less hassle with collecting the newspaper's share of the money and it was always well organised. Within a year I had given up my own paper round, handing it over to someone else. I was collecting money from customers on four or five rounds in the area. I was doing the part of the job that I loved, and my income had more than doubled. That was pretty cool, and I continued doing that for several years until *The Daily Colonist* merged with the other newspaper in town and they changed their whole approach to delivery and collections.

That was my first exposure to the world of mergers and acquisitions.

In the spring of 1974, just before my twelfth birthday, my parents took my sister (who was sixteen) and me on a holiday to Europe. Little did our parents know it would be the spark that would lead to huge changes in both my sister's life and mine. We landed at Heathrow airport and travelled into central London, a city that I quickly fell in love with and am still in love with today. A city that I have proudly called my home since 1993.

After a week in London, we travelled to the continent, visiting France, Germany and the Netherlands. I was fascinated, but frustrated – fascinated by the different architecture, cars, fashion, food and everything that gives a culture its own unique identity; frustrated by one thing: I couldn't communicate with people.

When we returned home, I started high school. In Canada, it is compulsory to learn both English and French, and I was really drawn to learning a new language because I could picture how life was different in France and I was beginning to have a grasp on how language plays such a critical role in creating cultural identity. A year later, I started to learn German as well.

In 1976, my first exposure to fundraising was taking out a bank loan. That year, Canada hosted the Summer Olympics in Montreal. Canada is a big country and Montreal is about 3,000 miles from Victoria, but the whole country was gripped with excitement. I had recently become interested in numismatics (collecting coins) and the Royal Canadian Mint had just announced a special series of coins to commemorate the 1976 Olympics. The full set of coins, which were offered in a collector's presentation box that included a $20 gold coin and a specially printed dollar bill, was on sale for $300. I really wanted this for my coin collection, but I only had $100 in savings.

I remember talking with my dad about this, and he said that he would take me to see his bank manager to talk about getting a loan so I could buy the coins. Dad explained to me how loans worked: that I would have to make monthly repayments and that there was an interest charge to pay as well. We made an appointment with the local bank (back when banks actually had branch managers who made loans – but that's another story). I got dressed up in my best clothes and went downtown with Dad to meet his bank manager.

I told the bank manager about the coin set that I wanted to buy, and that I had $100 saved up but needed an additional $200. I told him that I had a steady income from the newspaper collections and that I could afford to pay back $10 a month. We talked about how I managed my money, how I had saved up the $100 and why it was important to me to buy the coin set. Out came the forms, which I signed (and Dad countersigned), and presto! My bank account had $300 in it and I was able to buy the coin set.

That was my first acquisition.

I have a crystal clear memory of walking back to the car with Dad, and him saying to me, 'Now, David, there is one important thing you need to remember. What you borrow, you must pay back.' Those words have stuck with me throughout my life. Over the next two years I made sure to put at least $10 into the bank account every month to repay the loan. I didn't know it at the time, but when I turned sixteen, I had a good credit rating.

In 1977, my whole family (I am the youngest of four children) took a trip to Europe. My sister, who had been with us on that first trip, had gone back to Europe when she finished school. She met a man in Holland with whom she fell in love. They got married and settled down in a small town just outside Rotterdam. The whole family went to see them in their new life.

At this point I had finished three years of learning French and two years of German. Returning to Europe allowed me to put my schooling to the test in the real world. My language skills were far from fluent, but they were enough to communicate – to understand and to be understood. It opened my mind to a world of possibility. At the age of fifteen, I set my first life goal, even though at the time I didn't know what a life goal was. I decided that one day I would live in Europe.

Fast forward to the summer of 1982, just before my twentieth birthday. I was at university and had a summer job as a bank teller, working for the Royal Bank of Canada. This was about the time that banks started putting in the first generation ATMs (automatic teller (or cash) machines), so the norm was for customers to come into the bank, queue up and deposit or withdraw money. It was my third summer working for the bank, and the branch manager decided to give me some extra responsibility, so I was made the coin teller. This meant I had the biggest safe in the vault, as I had to store all of the coins that the branch held. It wasn't a huge amount of money, but coins take up a lot of space.

One day, right after a bank holiday weekend, I came into work to discover the senior teller was off sick. Normally, all of the tellers had a float of up to $10,000 and anything in excess was held by the senior teller. As she was off sick, the excess cash had to be stored in my safe that night, as it was the only one big enough to hold it. The Tuesday after the long weekend had been particularly busy and several large retail customers had come in with big deposits from all their weekend takings. I remember cashing up that night and realising that I had custody of over half a million dollars in cash. That was pretty heady stuff for a kid aged just nineteen. More clearly than that, though, I remember standing in the vault holding $100,000 in cash in my hands: ten bundles of one hundred $100 bills. It was mind-blowing.

A year later, I graduated from university with a Bachelor of Arts degree in Economics and German. I had always been good with numbers, and after flirting with a career in banking, I decided that the better route would be to train as a Chartered Accountant. It was a competitive field, just like today, and in 1983 in Victoria there were only eight jobs on offer and over 1,000 people applying. I was offered a job with Price Waterhouse (now part of PwC), one of the most prestigious firms.

A few months after joining, I learned what had set me apart from all the other applicants. The reason I got the job was because I spoke German. Unbeknown to me, Price Waterhouse had recently acquired a large accounting firm with offices in Germany, Austria and Switzerland. They were desperate for Anglo-Saxon qualified accountants who spoke the language. I qualified in May 1987. Two months later, my wife and I boarded the first of three planes that would take us from Victoria to Vancouver to London, and on to Zürich. We spent six years in Zürich before moving to London in 1993, and have lived here ever since.

After leaving the accounting profession, I worked for blue-chip companies like AT&T and the BBC. My experience with acquisitions evolved when I joined an acquisitive New York based PR agency network as European chief financial officer (CFO). I then went on to be the CFO of a couple of businesses listed on the Alternative Investment Market (AIM) of the London Stock Exchange. Over the course of my career I have raised over £100 million in debt and equity funding and bought or sold more than twenty companies. Big, exciting strategic stuff, but I reached a point in 2010 where it was no longer fulfilling, and I quit my job to launch a new business.

Fast forward to today, and I work exclusively with entrepreneurs, showing them how to raise money and grow their businesses exponentially with a view to exiting. The culmination of all those life experiences showed that the traditional rules of organic growth can be changed, and the FACE methodology evolved from that. It's not something that's just for big business. It can be applied to any business and any entrepreneur who is willing to change the rules.

Chapter wrap

In this chapter we've covered:

- Key moments growing up that shaped the person I have become
- My first experiences of fundraising and acquisitions as a child
- How the FACE methodology evolved from those life experiences

More than anything else, the thing I want you to take away from this chapter is to accept the challenge from Viktor Frankl and carry out your concrete assignment that demands fulfilment.

4

Case Study: Huveaux

Before getting into the details of the FACE methodology, I want to share with you the story of a company that I was CFO of for three years. I was a main board director and a shareholder too.

During that time we achieved these growth statistics:

- Sales grew from £1.1 million to £27.7 million (25×)

- Pre-tax profits grew from £0.4 million to £4.3 million (11×)

- Staff grew from twenty-three to 285 people (12×)

These are all numbers that are in the public domain because it is a company listed on AIM.

A credible business plan, a credible entrepreneur

In 2002, I was introduced to a man named John van Kuffeler. He was the chairman of a FTSE-100 company and had recently changed from being executive chairman to non-executive chairman of that company. This meant he had a lot more free time, so he founded a company called Huveaux plc (pronounced Hugh-Vo).

John is an entrepreneur who brings a unique set of large company skills, contacts and experience to the game. Like any entrepreneur, John decided to start Huveaux from scratch. He saw the way the world was changing and decided to start a digital media and publishing business.

What sets John apart is that he began with a clear vision: to build a substantial publishing and digital media group over the next ten to fifteen years. To do this, he needed to have serious money at his disposal.

Ambitious, visionary entrepreneurs often talk about building their companies to the point where they can do an initial public offering (IPO) when the company is listed on a stock exchange. That is their exit strategy. Because of his skills, contacts and experience, John was able to list the company before it began trading. He planted the seeds of the exit – for himself and all future shareholders – by the fact that the shares of

Huveaux plc were listed on AIM and could be bought and sold on a daily basis.

In its early days, the company was what is called a cash shell. It was a listed company that had £3 million in cash but no other trade or business. John was able to raise that money from private and institutional investors because they believed in his business plan and in him. Remember, he was also the chairman of a FTSE-100 company.

It will be the same for you when it comes time to raise money. Investors will have to believe in your business plan, and more importantly they will have to believe in you.

Buy-and-build strategy

Let's go back to John and Huveaux. John's plan was what is referred to as a buy-and-build strategy. Because the company was listed on a stock exchange, John had access to raising capital by selling equity. He certainly didn't 'give' any equity away.

About a year after the business launched, John made his first acquisition. He bought a political publishing company called Vacher-Dod, which had a heritage dating back to the early 19th century, for £4.5 million. As part of the deal, John went back to the stock exchange and raised another £2.5 million in cash. He had £3 million from the IPO plus £2.5 million from this raise, so in total he had £5.5 million to spend. Of this, £4.5 million went to the owners of Vacher-Dod. This left the company with £1 million in cash.

I'll always remember one of the first things John said to me when we met: 'I sleep better at night knowing there's a million pounds in the bank.'

In early 2003, John invited me to join the HQ team at Huveaux. I had the honour and privilege of being the company's first CFO. That year, we raised £14.5 million on the stock exchange and made three acquisitions.

The first acquisition was an educational publishing company called Lonsdale. It was a really nice business that had been started by two former high-school teachers who saw a gap in the market and wrote revision guides to help kids study for their exams. We raised £7 million by selling shares at 25p to fund the deal, which cost £6.9 million. The owners of Lonsdale were paid £4.9 million in cash at completion, with deferred consideration, subject to future growth of the Lonsdale business (more on that in the chapter A is for Acquire).

Lonsdale was a wonderful little business. The founders worked from home and wrote the first revision guides themselves. Later they engaged a number of specialist teachers to help write revision guides, which they edited to a house style. They had a sales and administration office that ran from a former NHS nursing station in the back of a car park in a small town in Lancashire and a warehouse in Carlisle.

What set the company apart was that Lonsdale's revision guides exactly matched the published school curriculum. When a new guide was written, the company would send one copy by post to the lead subject teacher at every high school in their database, along with an order form. The orders piled in. It was a classic case of a product that exactly meets what the customer wants, offered at an attractive price and sold in volume. More than a million revision guides were sold the year we bought Lonsdale. The sales and cash flowed with the usual school cycles.

The second deal was a French political publishing business called Le Trombinoscope. It was owned by a big French publishing group that was focusing its business on the beauty and wine industries, and 'Trombi', as it was called, no longer fitted its model. It was perfect for us, because Huveaux now had leading political publishing companies in the UK and France. This was a smaller deal, valued at £1.6 million, funded from existing cash in the business.

Much like the Vacher-Dod business in the UK, Le Trombinoscope was connected into the highest levels of the French political scene. One year at the annual Le Trombinoscope Awards evening, a certain Monsieur Sarkozy stopped by with his entourage. This was about a year before he became President of France, so he was like royalty in a republican French way. It was fascinating to observe.

Trombi was the first deal I did on my own. From start to finish, I led the whole acquisition process. Completion of the deal was dragging on and August was fast approaching. The whole of France shuts down for August, and I go back to Canada for a month to visit family and friends.

The first three days of my holiday, which started at the end of July, were spent completing the acquisition. I remember there was one contentious issue that needed a lot of discussion before we could agree the deal. We were on a call at 3pm in Paris, which is 6am on the west coast of Canada. It was a conference call with the vendors and lawyers, and I was walking up and down the beach in front of my parents' home because everyone else was asleep.

All of a sudden, a flock of a dozen or so Canada Geese flew overhead making all the noise those birds can make. And then it was gone. When I explained to the people in Paris what had just happened, they thought it was hilarious. It broke the deadlock. We sorted out the last sticking point and the deal was agreed.

At this stage John and I recruited the first person into my team at head office to support us on future deals. The workload was intense, and we needed a team to make this happen. It would have been incredibly difficult to continue growing like we did without bringing skilled people on board.

The final acquisition that year was another education business (are you starting to see the theme?) called Fenman, which published a magazine called *Training Journal* and a range of videos and manuals focused on the adult education market. The deal cost £6.2 million. To fund this, we raised £7.5 million at 35p a share. The market value of Huveaux had grown and the investors who'd bought in at the Lonsdale deal, when we raised money at 25p a share, were now sitting on a 40% increase in the value of their holding. They didn't mind their percentage stake being diluted, and some of them increased their stake to support us.

The chap who would be hired to run the UK business had not joined us yet, and as I was the only other executive director of Huveaux at the time, the integration of the Fenman business fell to me. I learned a great deal about the publishing industry thanks to Fenman and its team of people. It was hugely beneficial.

John created Huveaux with a vision of building a substantial publishing and digital media group over a period of ten to fifteen years. At the end of 2003, just two years into operation, the group comprised:

- The largest publisher of political biographical information in the EU

- The publication and sale of more than a million school revision guides

- Three magazines

- Three subscription websites

- The production and sale of twenty-two training videos and more than 100 training manuals for the adult education market

In one year, revenue had grown fourfold from £1.1 million to £4.6 million, with pre-tax profits trebling from £0.4 million to £1.2 million. Try doing that with organic growth! And that was just the beginning.

In 2004 we hired two senior executives who joined the board of directors. They had both spent many years running publishing businesses, and we needed their skills and experience as we started the year with four companies employing sixty-four people in two countries. This was a critical move in terms of strengthening the team, because it meant the UK businesses (Vacher-Dod, Lonsdale and Fenman) and Le Trombinoscope each had appropriate experienced leaders. We also hired a financial controller who took over most of the day-to-day finance responsibilities in head office. This enabled the rest of the head office team to focus on raising more money and doing more acquisitions. That year we raised £17 million on the stock exchange and acquired three more companies – starting and ending with two little ones, and a big one in the middle.

The first deal was to buy a publication called *Public Affairs Newsletter*, which was the trade rag for the lobbying industry in the UK and Europe. It sat nicely with our expanding political publishing business. We bought *Public Affairs Newsletter* for £0.8 million, funded from existing cash resources.

From an operational perspective, this business dropped into Vacher-Dod. We had a source of journalists for content. We had our own editorial team. We gave it to the team and it carried on as a subscription-based product. Recurring revenue is always a good thing and we liked subscription-based products that were easy to make using our existing staff, systems and processes.

ATP Egora

The last deal that year is the smallest acquisition I have ever made. It is also unquestionably the best one. ATP Egora was an online and print publisher of medical magazines in France. It had been acquired by France Telecom in 2001 when that company was gobbling up everything internet related it could get its hands on. By 2004, ATP Egora was a tiny and seemingly irrelevant part of a huge national telecoms firm, and France Telecom decided to sell it.

Enter Huveaux plc. Because it had been owned by a huge corporate for a few years, ATP Egora's small balance sheet included a mess of transactions related to corporate recharges and expenses that were nothing to do with the medical publishing business. The deal was agreed on the basis that we would acquire ATP Egora on a debt-free, cash-free basis, which meant France Telecom had to wipe out the corporate recharges from the balance sheet and could keep any cash that was in the business.

On completion day, I took the train to Paris with a banker's draft for €500,000 in my briefcase. At a meeting in a small office in southwest Paris, I handed over the €500,000 and France Telecom gave me the share certificates. Huveaux now owned the company.

I went to the ATP Egora offices and sat down with the managing director and the financial controller, asking to see that morning's bank statement. The balance in the bank was €513,000. France Telecom had cleaned up the group liabilities that were on the books, but had forgotten to take out the cash. In effect, we took ownership of the business for free, plus €13,000 in cash.

Some people might question the ethics of this. France Telecom had clearly made a mistake and we profited from it. Having spent my early career in big corporates,

I am sure that the executives who were handling the sale of ATP Egora would have had to take this back up the chain of command to approve the bank transfer, which could have been embarrassing to them and harmed their careers, but in the context of a huge corporation like France Telecom, it was a rounding difference. For that reason, we chose to quietly benefit from their mistake. Had this been an acquisition from an individual or a small business, I have no doubt the decision would have been different.

The deal gets even better.

Because of the various corporate costs that France Telecom had charged to ATP Egora, it had racked up tax losses that existed after the clean-up. But this was a publishing business, so France Telecom couldn't use the losses against its telecoms profits. We already had a profitable publishing business in France and were able to structure the deal in a way that let us offset the accumulated losses in ATP Egora against the profits we made from Trombi (and in later years from another French acquisition). That meant we were able to recover a further €0.3 million in tax from the French authorities.

When all was said and done, we had a third division to the business (political, educational and now medical). We effectively got it for free plus €13,000 in cash, and we recovered €300,000 of tax paid by our other French business. The best deal I have ever done, bar none.

We also built the team further. The financial controller at ATP Egora took over responsibility for finance at Le Trombinoscope from the publishing house we had acquired it from.

Buying a competitor

Sandwiched between those two little deals, we completed our first eight-figure acquisition, a company called Parliamentary Communications. This was our main (and much bigger) competitor in the UK political publishing market, and it also had a presence in Brussels. We bought it for £16.2 million, funding the acquisition by raising £16.8 million at 50p a share.

The shareholders who backed the Lonsdale deal and invested at 25p had doubled their money. The ones who came in with the Fenman deal were sitting on a 43% gain. Nobody minded their percentage stake being diluted because the value of their holding had increased. More importantly, this deal made us the unquestioned leader of political publishing in the UK and EU.

The acquisition also brought an established finance team, and the finance director of Parliamentary Communications was soon promoted to that role for the whole UK business as we continued to strengthen our team.

Unlike Vacher-Dod, which was staid, small-c conservative and had a tradition dating back to the early 19th century, Parliamentary Communications was the brash new kid on the block. It was a sales-driven organisation, and over a short period of time built its main publication, *House Magazine*, and its website www.epolitix.com to be leading sources of news and information about the UK parliamentary scene. It also ran training courses for the civil service.

We merged the two companies under the Dods brand because it had the greater heritage and recognition. The Parliamentary Communications team were delighted to be able to speak to customers using Dods branding.

I remember just after the 2005 general election, there were a couple of seats where there had to be vote recounts. No information had been provided on these results, and a few days after the election, our team of researchers contacted the House of Commons to find out what the results had been. Our team was told that no one knew, and the person at the House of Commons suggested that we might try contacting Dods for the answer. It was beautiful irony.

A few days before completion of the Parliamentary Communications deal, there was an unusual jump in our share price, which spiked up to 77.5p one day, accompanied by increased volume of shares traded. The first thing that entered my head was: 'There's been a leak'. Insider trading is a serious crime and sadly one that is alive and well in the shadows.

Thankfully, that wasn't the case. A few hours later we found out that we'd been recommended as a buy on an online stock tipping service. It knew nothing about the Parliamentary Communications deal and had simply recommended Huveaux to its readers as a company that was going places.

At the end of 2004, we had strengthened the board of directors, established strong finance leaders and restructured operations to meet the needs of a growing business that now had:

- Trebled sales from £4.6 million to £14.4 million

- Doubled pre-tax profit from £1.2 million to £2.4 million (and don't forget the French tax benefits from the ATP Egora deal which had a big impact below the pre-tax line)

- Operations in three countries – the UK, France and Belgium

- More than doubled staff numbers from 64 to 139

And it keeps going.

An Epic deal

In 2005 we made two substantial acquisitions, both of which had new features: each deal included debt funding for the first time (one fully and the other in part), and one of them was the takeover of another public company listed on AIM. The latter meant we had to follow the rules laid down by the Takeover Panel, which regulates mergers and takeovers of companies listed on the London Stock Exchange. Not only that, we ran both deals simultaneously, which meant we needed to recruit two more people experienced in doing deals into the head office team.

The other AIM-listed company was called Epic Group plc. It was an e-learning business at a time when e-learning was just starting to get hot, and there's an interesting story as to how we acquired it.

In the spring of 2005, John and I were doing the rounds to see our institutional shareholders after the release of Huveaux's annual results for 2004. One of them also happened to be the largest shareholder in Epic, and they weren't entirely happy with the Epic management team who seemed to be holding back on growth, despite the fact that Epic had £10 million in the bank. After some discussion, they suggested that we should have a look at Epic and that they would support us making a bid for the company.

We took this back to our board and had lengthy discussions before deciding to proceed. We then spoke with our solicitors and auditors because we knew we were entering regulated territory and we had to follow the rules to the letter. It made the deal costs significantly higher because we had to involve our advisors at every step, from making initial contact through to the deal negotiation because both sides had to have their lawyers and brokers in on every single discussion between the two companies. We finally announced completion of the deal whereby the Epic shareholders exchanged their Epic shares for shares in Huveaux and some cash.

The Epic acquisition *was* epic. The deal was worth £25.2 million, and the owners of Epic received 32.6 million new shares in Huveaux plus £8.3 million in cash. We funded the cash element of the consideration by taking out a bridge loan (a large short-term debt facility) that was repaid post-acquisition from the cash that Epic had on its balance sheet.

Epic is the biggest acquisition I have ever made, and because of the Takeover Panel rules, it is also the most complicated. It was a massive learning experience. I'm going to make the bold assumption that most readers will not be acquiring a publicly traded company, and therefore will not need the details of complying with Takeover Panel rules. Suffice to say, if you do find yourself in this position, you will need to be working with highly skilled and qualified professional advisors who will make sure you do not fall foul of the rules.

Based in an old house near the seafront in Brighton, Epic was synonymous with the nascent UK e-learning industry. It was one of the first players in the market and helped to shape it during two decades by creating engaging, award-winning e-learning, blended learning and knowledge solutions. Epic had developed long-term relationships which helped to transform some of the UK's best-known private and public sector organisations, but it had historically restricted its business to bespoke applications for clients with no recurring revenue stream and little intellectual property. From the outset, our plan was to extend Epic's skills and experience, and to grow its revenue base by altering the approach and developing a portfolio of owned intellectual property to deliver a recurring revenue stream over the longer term.

JBB Santé

The second acquisition was another French healthcare business called Editions JB Ballière, also known as JBB Santé. It was owned by a French private equity house that wanted to re-focus its activities on large infrastructure projects, and a healthcare publishing business no longer fitted in its portfolio.

Because it was private equity owned, JBB Santé had a sizeable amount of debt on its balance sheet (that is a common way for private equity houses to fund deals – more on that in 'F Is For Fund' and Appendix 3). To pay for that deal, we took on a new term loan facility for £10 million.

This was a fascinating opportunity because a seismic shift was looming in the French healthcare world. Up to that point, there had been no compulsory continuing professional development (CPD) for doctors in France. The introduction of compulsory CPD meant the business model of the magazines was changing, shifting away from being advertiser funded to subscription based for qualifying CPD. That's a big change to a business model. Get it right and you're on to a winner, but it's not easy to get right. Customers who are used to free often don't want to pay.

At the end of the year we had again seen massive growth, both in the existing businesses and from the two new acquisitions. The results showed:

- Sales had almost doubled from £14.4 million to £27.7 million

- Pre-tax profit had grown from £2.4 million to £4.3 million

- Staff had more than doubled from 139 to 285

- We covered three solid sectors: political, education and healthcare

And all of that was achieved in just three years.

The year 2005 was possibly the busiest year of my life, running two deals at the same time, starting with the shareholder meetings in April when we first started looking at Epic through to August when that deal completed and then October when JBB Santé completed. And there was significant integration and consolidation work on both companies (more on that in C is for Consolidate). By the end of the year I decided it was time for a change and agreed with John to stand down from the board and resign as CFO after handing over to my successor.

Today, I'm still good friends with many of my former colleagues from Huveaux. We went through the trenches together, figuratively, and that forms deep bonds. I could not have completed this work, which played a core role in developing the FACE methodology, without the help and support from my team at head office and the finance teams in the UK and France businesses, as well as my colleagues on the board from whom I have learned so much. I am grateful to them all and thankful still to have John as one of my mentors.

PART TWO
THE FACE METHODOLOGY

5
F Is For Fund

'If you want to glide toward money, you have to make sure
your message is clear as a bell, and you need to ensure that
you have a unified team capable of communicating it.'
— Alejandro Cremades, Founder of crowdfunding
platform Rock the Post/Onevest and author of *The
Art of Startup Fundraising*

There is only one reason why a business fails. Well,
there may be two, but the second is because the
owner gives up on it. I'm going to make the bold
assumption that if you've read this far, you aren't the
type who would give up on the business.

The only reason a business fails is because it runs out
of money.

There are four main ways a business can get more money:

1. Increase sales revenue

2. Grant funding

3. Borrow money

4. Attract investors who buy a stake in the company

For many years, 1, 2 and 3 were the only ways for an SME to get more money. The first two are worth touching on here, but the real focus of this chapter is on items 3 and 4: borrowing money and attracting investors who buy a stake in the company. These are the ways you can fund a business with significant amounts of cash in a reasonably fast way.

Increased sales and grant funding

The way you increase sales revenue is by selling more of whatever product or service you offer, increasing the price of your product or service, or finding new products or services to add to the offering. Increasing sales revenue is the subject of many books, and there are hundreds of authors who are experts in marketing and sales with vastly more experience than I have in achieving that. If that is what you're looking for then I recommend you look elsewhere.

Grant funding is an interesting area that can provide real help to certain businesses, as long as they fit the criteria for the grant. The attraction of grant funding is that it is given away, with no requirement that the funder repay or return the money. The only expectation the grantor has is that the money is spent on the purpose for which the grant was applied. But that doesn't mean it comes with no strings attached.

Early in my career with Price Waterhouse, I was assigned to a job where I had to audit the files of a government department that was allocating tourism grants for small businesses operating in remote parts of British Columbia. Looking back, it wasn't really that surprising, but at the time I remember being astonished at the amount of compliance reporting that was required of the applicants before, during and after the completion of the grant application.

Again, grant funding is not my area of expertise. There are not anywhere near as many books about grant funding as there are about marketing and sales, but a quick search on Google should point you in the direction of advisors who can help you with a grant application.

Borrowing money and attracting investors to your company is my forte and that's what the rest of this chapter will focus on.

Getting started

Most SME businesses operate through a limited company. If the business you are running is not structured in this way and you want to use the FACE methodology, you need to change this.

Operating through a limited company makes sense on so many levels. It protects you legally by separating the business from you as an individual; it is often more tax efficient for paying yourself; for companies registered in the UK, it allows you to take advantage of some attractive tax breaks that you can offer to your investors (see Appendix 1 on the Enterprise Investment Scheme (EIS) and the Seed Enterprise Investment Scheme (SEIS)); and it's both easy and cheap. Setting up a limited company takes about fifteen minutes to do online and costs less than a round of drinks at the pub.

Next, you need to decide whether to take the debt or equity route when raising funds. There's an important distinction to make: when you borrow money, you have to pay it back. When you raise money by selling equity (shares in the limited company), the investor has an ownership stake in the business. You don't have to pay them back, but if the company pays dividends, the investors are entitled to their fair share. If you sell the business, they will be entitled to their percentage stake in the price you sell for.

Finally, you must have a robust, considered and thorough business plan. It should set out what the business is, where it is today and the direction you want to take it in. Keep it clear and simple. Identify milestones you want to work towards and include these in your plan. Clearly state how you will use the money you raise; this will not only give you clear goals, it will also enable potential investors to understand what the business is and where it's going. As Alejandro Cremades suggests in the quote at the beginning of the chapter, you need to ensure that your top team is fully behind the plan and that all of you can communicate it clearly and succinctly.

It is critically important to understand that when you raise funds, whether by taking on debt or selling equity in the company, you are granting someone else the right to have some say over how the business is run. It is also critically important that you seek professional advice as part of this process, particularly before you sign on the dotted line. You need good lawyers and accountants on your side.

Challenge the scarcity mindset

Thinking back to Chapter 2 – Your Head, I want you to get rid of any preconceptions you may have about scarcity. We live in challenging times to be sure, and the world faces many problems. Shortage of money is not one of them.

There are many issues surrounding money – in fact, I may well write another book all about that – but let's stick with this one for now. We live in some of the most affluent times in human history. There is more money out there than you can possibly imagine, and new forms of money are coming up all the time, like cryptocurrencies. Think abundance, because it's out there for the taking.

Now let me guide you through the juicy bits in detail and show you how.

Borrowing money

There are many ways to borrow money, and with the tightening of regulation on banks and the growth of new FinTech companies that is happening as I write, there are new players entering the debt-funding market all the time. Nonetheless, the fundamental concept of debt funding remains the same: party 1 (the lender) lends money to party 2 (the borrower) and they agree a structure by which party 2 will repay the money, plus interest. The lender may also take security over assets of the company, or assets of the owner(s) of the company (referred to as a personal guarantee – more on that later). In the event the borrower fails to repay the loan, the lender can take these assets and use or sell them to service the debt.

Over the course of my career, I have completed debt facilities from as small as $200 (when I was fourteen years old to buy my commemorative Olympic coins) to as large as £10 million, and in total I have raised about £30 million of debt funding in the UK, USA, Germany and Canada. I remember the words my dad spoke as we left the bank back in 1976: 'What you borrow, you must pay back.' If you don't, or if you breach certain terms of the loan agreement, this has serious negative implications, including:

- The company's credit rating will be impaired, making it harder to borrow money in future. With the widespread sharing of credit information, this news will be known to all institutional lenders and anyone who has access to credit agency reports.

- Loan agreements typically have default provisions which, among other things, often mean that the lender can charge a higher rate of interest while the loan is in default. Instead of, say, an 8% interest rate on the loan, the default rate might be 20%. It can quickly get expensive.

- The lender has the right to exercise their security charges. This means, for example, that they can take over the accounts receivable and collect them, starving the company of incoming cash. The lender can seize assets and sell them in the open market. They can make changes to the management of the company, including firing members of the executive team – including you.

- In extreme cases, the lender can wipe out the shareholders and take control of the equity. In one of the acquisitions I completed, the company was backed by a private equity house that had put in a sizeable loan. When the company defaulted, the loan facility agreement included a clause that meant the private equity house as debt holder ended up owning 99.99% of the fully diluted equity in the business. Everyone else's share – including that of the founders, other investors and even staff who had options – was wiped out.

Debt can be an incredibly powerful tool in your growth strategy. Just be sure that you do not default on the conditions of the loan. In addition to the repayment of principal and interest when it is due, you must also fully understand the reporting requirements and the covenants that are part of the facility agreement.

We'll take a look at each of those.

Reporting requirements and covenants

Reporting requirements are linked to providing your lender with regular financial information, typically in the form of monthly or quarterly management accounts, as well as the full financial statements after the end of each year. The lender may require you to have the financial statements audited, so watch out for that as well.

Generally the lender will want to receive copies of the management accounts within ten days of the end of each month or quarter, so be sure that your finance team has the ability to produce them within the required timeframe. Being late can trigger default provisions. Annual financial statements usually need to be submitted within ninety days of year-end. Depending on the nature of the business, there may be other metrics that the lender requires, and these will be set out in the facility agreement. There will also be things like reporting if you are ever threatened or served with litigation. Be aware of these and comply with them.

Moving on to covenants, which is lending-agreement speak for promises. Covenants fall into two types: positive and negative. Positive covenants are things that you must do, for example provide audited financial statements within ninety days of year-end, maintain agreed levels of insurance on the business and key people within it, or retain membership in whatever trade or professional association you may be a member of. Negative covenants are things you must not do, for example certain financial ratios, like total debt on the balance sheet must not exceed three times earnings before interest, taxes depreciation and amortisation (EBITDA), and debt servicing costs (the sum of all interest and principal payments over the next twelve months) must not be more than EBITDA, as well as non-financial covenants like not shutting down any operations or trade of the business, or the company may not pay any dividends or take on any other debt funding. These can be complex and I urge you to take professional advice whenever you enter into a loan agreement. Again, be aware of the covenants and comply with them.

Let's have a brief look at personal guarantees (PGs) as well. Particularly some of the FinTech companies that are springing up, while they do make it easier and faster to borrow money than the banks, they also want a 'PG', and if you refuse, you won't get funding from them. If you can in any way avoid granting a PG, please do.

The great thing about having a limited company is that it limits the liability to that legal entity. With relatively few exceptions, the shareholders of a limited company are protected from having to pay in any additional resources even if the company falls on hard times. This is sometimes referred to as the corporate veil. Granting a PG completely bypasses that, because the guarantor is putting their own assets (home, pension, savings, car, etc) on the line as part of the security for the debt. Lenders always want it if they can get it.

A final word of advice if you ever take on debt finance. If there are signs that something may be about to go wrong in the business, keep your lender informed.

Do not try to hide it. Be proactive and tell them. Many responsible lenders will work hard with their borrowers to ensure the loan stays current.

For example, during the financial crash in 2008–09, I was able to negotiate a waiver of covenants that would otherwise have been breached and put the facility into default. I was able to secure the waiver from the lender because I had kept an open and professional relationship with them and kept them fully informed as to what was happening in the business.

Crowdfunding

Crowdfunding enables companies to raise money from a large number of people – ie from 'the crowd'. Typically, investments range from £10 to tens of thousands. Crowdfunding has changed the rules of the fundraising game; some sites offer debt, some equity, and there are even sites where the business raising money can ask for donations or offer gifts in exchange.

One of the best-known debt crowdfunding sites in the UK is Funding Circle, www.fundingcircle.com. If you're looking for equity, the UK leader is Crowdcube, www.crowdcube.com. You only need to Google 'crowdfunding' to find a multitude of sites, which you can use to raise money.

Have a look at other companies that have raised money on the site. Learn what works and what doesn't by reviewing both companies that are doing well, and those that aren't succeeding. Perhaps their business plan is not sound, their video needs work or the market for their product doesn't exist.

Sites like Crowdcube have a serious vetting process, which includes testing your business plan and assessing whether there is, in fact, a market for your product. I have helped clients raise money with Crowdcube in the past and have been told that only one in three companies that applies actually passes the vetting stage. Statistics on the Crowdcube site indicate that 60% of companies that make it through are successful in completing their funding. I've also seen companies make it through the vetting stage but not complete their raise.

How does it work? It depends on the site. With Funding Circle, the crowd offers loans to the company, typically repayable with interest over three to five years, and loans are always backed by a PG from the entrepreneur. On Crowdcube, companies offer shares in exchange for money given by investors. Alternatively, sites like Kickstarter offer gifts in exchange for donations.

Provided it has a solid business plan and a clear vision, even the smallest startup can successfully raise money through crowdfunding. Perhaps you haven't made your product yet, but you are confident of the market.

As long as you have clearly laid out your plan and the milestones you hope to achieve, crowdfunding can be for you.

One entrepreneur I know made clever use of a donation crowdfunding site. She needed £5,000 to publish her book, so she offered different gifts depending on the level of investment. For £10 she would give the donor a signed copy of the book, for £100 a signed copy and invitation to the launch party, while a donation of £1,000 was rewarded with a credit in the book. This is a good way of raising smaller amounts of money with low risk for both investor and company.

A couple of years ago I helped a client secure a £100,000 loan on Funding Circle. We got all the details ready and submitted the application on a Monday. On Tuesday we had a call from one of the Funding Circle team to ask some questions, which we were able to answer straight away. On Wednesday they sent us the documentation, which we signed and returned. On Thursday our loan went live on the Funding Circle site, and on Friday the cash was in the bank. Debt crowdfunding really can work quickly.

Several years ago I raised £120,000 on Crowdcube for a client whose final product was not complete. We built the plan and had a base of customers lined up who had paid advance deposits towards the product that was being offered, but to make it happen we needed additional cash and decided to sell equity. It's not as fast as debt funding, but from start to finish it took just over three months until the cash was in the bank and the company completed the product. In the years that followed, that company raised a further £180,000 from the investors who had come in during the Crowdcube round.

According to the Crowdcube site, the most common sectors are Technology, Internet Business, and Food and Drink. Statistics on the site show that in 2018, the average amount raised was £1.1 million and 198 businesses succeeded in completing their raise. One company, Monzo, raised £20 million from 36,000 members of the crowd. You can aim for the stars. Just ensure your plans for growth reflect that.

By its nature, equity crowdfunding raises money through a multitude of investors. This, paired with the relatively low sums invested, means that companies tend to maintain a large degree of control. Businesses will have the names and contact information of their investors and will update them on progress and development, but essentially, they are not involved in the day-to-day business. The investors pay in money and are given loan notes, shares or gifts in return. This is in contrast to angel investors, venture capitalists and private equity firms who tend to have far more control over business strategy. More on that in a moment.

Done right, crowdfunding is an accessible way for SMEs to raise money through debt or equity, and to raise awareness at the same time.

Raising equity funding

To give the discussion about raising equity funding some context, I'm going to create a fictitious company called ABC Limited, which is owned by three partners, Annabel, Brian and Charlie.

Through their own resources, supplemented with money from friends and family, the three founders set up ABC with £30,000 in cash and each is issued with 10,000 shares. ABC is a tech business which has developed a product it is now bringing to market using the software as a service (SaaS) business model. It needs more money to make this happen so the founders decide to seek external equity investment.

There are four main sources of equity funds that become relevant as the company grows:

- Angel investors
- Venture capital
- Private equity
- Public markets

In the following sections, we will start with the theory and practice, followed by the story of Annabel, Brian and Charlie, and how ABC Limited evolves and develops as it goes through each type of investment.

Angel investors

Angel investing is the next step up from crowdfunding – the sums are greater, the investor involvement is higher and it is slightly trickier to access, but the payoff from a successful relationship with an angel can be huge. Typically, angels operate in networks and several members will team up to make investments in qualifying companies, usually up to £500,000.

Angel investors are typically wealthy individuals who have a background in business and investment. Often, they are entrepreneurs themselves who have sold a business and want to invest their money in companies they perceive to have a good trajectory for growth. But it's not just about the cash; angels will get involved in the strategic decisions of your company, lend their expertise and open up their book of contacts to your business.

Done correctly, investment via an angel can propel your business towards great success and help you achieve the growth of your dreams.

NIGEL JOINS AS THE ANGEL INVESTOR

Annabel, Brian and Charlie put together a business plan showing that, with an investment of £250,000, they would be able to garner significant market share and establish ABC as a leader in its sector. They know what to spend the money on and what needs to happen to deliver a strong return.

Annabel knows a member of the UK Business Angels Association, the trade body for angel investors, and she reaches out to them. This contact suggests they start by researching a number of angel investor networks and making contact with the main coordinator of the ones that appear most relevant to them. Networks are formed of a group of angel investors, and they typically have one person who acts as the coordinator. This individual may or may not be an investor, but they are of critical importance as they are the gatekeeper to the network.

After searching on Google, Annabel, Brian and Charlie identify seven angel networks that might be a good fit with ABC and start digging further into them. It is sometimes difficult to get all the information as angel networks can be quite secretive, but in the end they manage to identify the gatekeepers at four angel networks. They do more research on these four, but through LinkedIn are only able to identify contacts in their networks who could introduce them to two of the gatekeepers.

Undaunted, they approached all four – two with an email introduction from mutual contacts and the other two cold. They are able to secure appointments to speak with both of the introduced gatekeepers and one of the others. Following pre-qualifying calls with the three gatekeepers, Annabel, Brian and Charlie are invited to pitch ABC's investment case to two networks.

Annabel, Brian and Charlie spend the next few weeks rehearsing their pitch presentation and trying to anticipate the kinds of questions they may be asked. When the dates for their pitches arrive, they are ready. Depending on the angel network, they find themselves pitching to anywhere from eight to fifteen people. In some regards it feels like they are on the television show *Dragon's Den*, although there are no piles of cash on the table nor dramatic music in the background.

The pitches go well and they have interest from both networks. They are particularly attracted to one of them, where a chap named Nigel has a background in technology and is experienced in the industry their product is targeted at. It looks like a match made in heaven – no wonder they are called angels.

The deal is negotiated between ABC and Nigel, who is representing the network. In the end ABC secures the full £250,000, with Nigel investing £150,000 and two other members of the network putting in £50,000 each. Nigel is appointed as a director of the company and works closely with the three founders over the next two years as the business grows and develops.

It isn't always smooth sailing. Development of the technology takes nearly twice as long as anticipated and that puts a serious burden on ABC's cash flow. Nigel remains supportive of the business, but for nearly six months he really turns up the heat on Annabel, Brian and Charlie to get the situation under control.

Once things recover and the business is back on track, Nigel agrees to open his little black book and make a number of introductions that will be hugely beneficial to ABC. By the end of the second year, the business is growing ahead of plan and the angels are very pleased.

Venture capital

Now we turn to the institutional side of things. When you're dealing with venture capital (VC), private equity (PE) or public markets, the vast majority of the investors are institutions that manage other people's money. They may well invest some of their own alongside, but most of the money in these firms is being managed on behalf of their clients. Because of this, the checks are tougher and the investor involvement is higher.

VC is incredibly competitive, with many VC firms receiving hundreds of proposals each year. For this reason, an introduction to the firm is extremely beneficial. VCs tend to specialise in a specific industry. It may be that they invest in FinTech, media, or healthcare related businesses, but their focus tends to be narrow, and each will have an expert in the field. This person will be brought in to dissect and challenge your business plan, so it must be rock solid. Companies generally raise between £250,000 and £5 million using VC firms, so although the risk is high for both company and investor, the growth potential is tremendous.

With unsolicited or unintroduced plans, it's not uncommon for the most junior member of the firm to have a checklist and spend five to ten minutes (sometimes less time) skimming through your business plan to assess whether you qualify for investment.

You must grab their attention in this time, which can be difficult. For this reason, it is a good idea to find someone you know to introduce you to a firm instead.

The VC firm will structure the investment deal in a way that protects its interests over everyone else's, to ensure it get its money first. The way it achieves this is via a combination of common stock and preference shares or debt. This can get technical, so if you want to know more please check out Appendix 2. The main thing to take away is that VC firms will have a significant say in the business. Two other technical areas that will likely come up in all of these funding situations are valuation and shareholder agreements. These are dealt with in more detail in Appendix 3 and Appendix 4, respectively.

If things go according to plan, venture capitalists can be incredibly useful. Depending on the VC firm you are with, if the business grows according to plan, it can be easy to raise even more money to grow further and faster. Serial entrepreneurs who have had success with a firm can often go back and ask for more money to grow the company or to invest in their newest venture, once they have exited their previous one.

CHANGES AS ABC SECURES VC FUNDING

A few years after Nigel and his network invested in ABC, the business is growing well and the founding team decides to expand the company by targeting a new industry vertical that is showing great potential. Nigel is supportive of this move, but his angel network doesn't have access to the £1 million that ABC requires to make it. Fortunately, Nigel has good contacts into a leading technology VC firm, which funded one of his early ventures and did well from the deal. Nigel is able to secure a meeting with his friend Rebecca, who is one of the partners in that firm. This is hugely beneficial, since none of the founders has any VC contacts.

Knowing that VC firms are data hungry, Nigel is able to guide the founders in putting together a compelling presentation with the level of detail he knows Rebecca and her colleagues will want to see. They meet at the VC's offices. Rebecca is there with another partner, three analysts and a person who is introduced as the VC firm's technology expert. And expert he is, with PhDs from both Cambridge and MIT. Every technology deal this VC firm considers at partner level has to be passed by him before it will make the investment.

It is a gruelling meeting with detailed questions coming from every conceivable angle, and at the end Rebecca says she will get back to ABC within a few days. The wait is agonising. The expert gave nothing away when the ABC representatives answered his questions. He was stone-faced and spoke in a soft monotone. The other members of the VC team had also been at pains to appear neutral throughout the meeting. Nigel tries to reassure them the pitch went well, but Annabel, Brian and Charlie are anxious. They have never been subjected to that level of scrutiny or questioning before and have no idea whether it will be a yay or a nay.

Three days later, Rebecca rings with good news. The VC firm is interested in making the full £1 million investment, but she and her colleagues are challenging the valuation of ABC and want a bigger stake than they have been offered. After lengthy discussions between the founders, Nigel and his co-investors, they agree to accept the indicative offer.

The next step is for the VC firm to conduct due diligence. Nigel has warned the founders that ABC will be carrying the cost of that, and they have already set aside funds to cover it. Representatives from top law and accountancy firms show up at ABC and crawl all over the books for two weeks. The technology expert spends several days going through ABC's code and plans for developing the product for the new industry vertical.

ABC passes the due diligence and the terms of the investment are agreed. As part of the deal, the VC firm appoints an independent chairman of the board from its network of approved chairs, and Rebecca also joins the board of ABC.

The business continues to grow successfully over the next several years. It is a real adjustment for the founders, though, because the company has to 'grow up' very quickly. Things become much more formal: there are monthly board meetings, and the independent chairman is a stickler for ensuring the board operates properly, distributing comprehensive packs a week before each meeting which he expects everyone to read and digest so they can have meaningful discussions as a board. Early on, Charlie makes the mistake of not reading the pack before a board meeting and is unable to answer a number of key questions that come up in the discussions. Following the board meeting, Charlie is invited to a private meeting with the chairman. That mistake never happens again.

Private equity

Like venture capitalists, PE firms will pool money from wealthy investors and manage it in a professional fund. Unlike venture capitalists, PE firms are risk averse and tend to invest in established businesses that have a proven track record.

PE firms will not deal with early stage companies. Unless you are a really established entrepreneur, it is unlikely they will be on your immediate investment horizon. However, if you have had success with a VC firm and achieved solid growth, they may take on your business and help you expand into realms you hadn't ever imagined.

To successfully raise money with a PE firm, the business will need to demonstrate good profits, several years' worth of audited financial statements and a solid management team. You will also need a high turnover: anywhere from £10 million a year and up. As well as this, you will need a connection into the PE firm. They don't receive hundreds of applications a year, like some VC firms, but PE firms are still incredibly hard to get into.

PRIVATE EQUITY BACKING AND A NEW CEO

Six years later, ABC has grown into a substantial firm and Nigel and his network partners decide they want to realise the considerable gains they have made from their investment.

As angel investors, they like the thrill of early stage businesses. Rebecca's VC firm has also seen a significant return on investment, and as the fund it invested from is nearing maturity, it is keen to sell its stake and return cash to its investors.

Annabel, Brian and Charlie all want to stay with ABC, but have come to the realisation that none of them wants to be the chief executive of a company that has sales revenues of nearly £28 million and more than 100 staff. They want to find someone else who has the skills and experience to run the business now that it has grown.

Rebecca and the chairman agree to conduct a search for an experienced technology CEO who is interested in buying into an established business and taking it to the next level. After a few months they find Jeremy, who has an impressive track record and has recently exited from a deal with an SaaS business in a completely different industry sector. Jeremy and the PE house that backed him have sold that business to one of the global tech companies, and both are flush with cash.

Due diligence is not dissimilar to what ABC experienced when the VC firm invested, so everyone is well prepared for it, having lived under the strict adherence to governance rules the chairman has insisted upon. They agree a deal whereby Jeremy comes in as the new CEO of ABC and buys a 7% stake in the company. Annabel, Brian and Charlie hold 14% each, and the PE house acquires the remaining 51% from the angels and Rebecca's VC firm.

Rebecca, Nigel and the chairman all resign from the board. A new independent chairman is appointed, along with a new CFO whom the PE house has worked with before. Two of the partners from the PE house join the board as well.

Things go smoothly for a couple of years, until the next economic downturn and a global recession that lasts more than a year. Two of ABC's large customers go bust and many more have to rein in their expenditure. ABC's revenues are off nearly 20% compared to plan and the board acts swiftly to implement a serious cost-cutting programme.

Jeremy is decisive and puts forward a plan to cut costs by 30% in order to ensure ABC can survive the economic downturn. This is a new experience for Annabel, Brian and Charlie. Not since the first dip after Nigel joined the business have they had to face such a challenge, and certainly not at this scale. It is hard. They have to make some difficult decisions and let go of several employees who have been with them from the beginning. They know it is right for ABC, but it is the hardest thing the three founders have had to do.

The downturn brings opportunities as well. Several competitors are struggling having not reacted as quickly as ABC to the changing climate. The PE house has deep pockets, and after some discussions, the executive team decides to put forward an acquisition strategy to the board. Over the next twelve months, ABC raises more money from the PE house and buys three of its largest competitors, becoming the unquestioned number one SaaS business in several vertical markets.

Public markets

The last and largest source of raising funds is public markets. Raising money on the stock exchange is arguably the pinnacle of a privately held company's achievement; to list on the stock exchange means not only have you achieved incredible growth, but the business is worth a great deal.

For this, companies will tend to have a valuation of £20 million or more; anything smaller and the stock market probably isn't right. It can be a fantastic way of raising large sums of money, as we saw in the Huveaux case study, but there are a lot of regulations in place that you must follow, and they come with costs.

For UK based companies, AIM is a tried and tested route. It's been in existence for over twenty years and has more than 1,000 businesses listed. NASDAQ (National Association of Securities Dealers Automated Quotations) Stockholm is another option for the European market, as well as NASDAQ itself in the USA. To keep things simple, we'll stay focused on AIM.

Every company that lists on AIM is required to have a nominated advisor, or 'nomad'. These are specialist firms that have been approved by the London Stock Exchange – corporate finance advisors with solid knowledge and experience of dealing with companies that are coming to the market. Once you have made the decision for the company to join AIM, the first step is to appoint a nomad to guide you through the details of the listing process. After listing, the nomad continues to play an important role, advising the company on all matters associated with its shares and compliance with the rules of the stock exchange.

You will also need to appoint a stockbroker and suitable firms of solicitors, accountants and investor relations advisors who already have clients listed on

AIM. Stockbrokers must be members of the London Stock Exchange, and it is their role to manage and promote the trade of the company's shares on the stock market. In many cases, the nomad and stockbroker will be the same firm, but it is not a requirement. All of these advisors come at a cost, and the company must be sure to set aside funds to cover them.

To gain a listing, the company and its advisors must prepare an Admission Document, which sets out details about the company, its directors, the business strategy and three years of historical audited financial information. Unlike PE or VC deals, which include detailed financial projections, the company does not publish any forward-looking financial information. The rest of the Admission Document is essentially a business plan which sets out where the company is going, what it plans to do with the money and what the risk factors are.

Because it's a public market, there are regulations in place which clearly divide company and investor to avoid insider trading. The investors will receive regular communications and be invited to formal meetings when the company publishes its half-year and annual results, but they are not involved with the day-to-day, nor do they have a seat on the board.

Investors will rely on the UK combined code, which, among other things, requires listed businesses to have a certain number of non-executive directors on the board. These people will be required to have experience in public markets, with a solid track record and the ability to make independent decisions. The chairman is also key; they are responsible for running the board so must be independent from the chief executive. As well as this, every year the shareholders will be invited to an annual meeting, but unless you are a large, well-known company, it is unlikely that more than a dozen people will show up.

Raising money via public markets can be a fruitful route, yet it is highly regulated. If you have a public company, you will be required to publish a certain amount of information, and this must be done through the stock exchange's regulatory news service. Anything that could have an impact on the price of the company's shares, such as changes in directors and the publication of financials, must be communicated immediately to the stock exchange.

AN ALTERNATIVE TO THE PE APPROACH – GOING FOR IPO

Annabel, Brian and Charlie have all stayed with ABC, and now see an opportunity to realise their dream of making ABC a public company. They approach the board to discuss this and are told the investors want to look at valuations by both sale to a PE house and listing on AIM. The investors have no preference for one or the other, but they want the maximum cash return. After engaging advisors to look at alternatives, they take the decision to list the company on AIM.

The first step is to engage the nomad, who guides them through the entire listing process, starting with the Admission Document. The nomad asks about non-executive directors and learns ABC has always had directors representing the investors. But it's different on AIM. Non-executives are truly independent from the company, and while they may hold a small stake, they have a duty of care to all investors.

Nigel agrees to stay on as a non-executive, and the company finds an experienced chairman who has recently retired from being CEO of another listed company. In the end, ABC has seven directors: Annabel, Brian and Charlie are the executives, while the chairman, Nigel and two others are non-executive directors.

Next, the board appoints a top City law firm which specialises in taking companies on to AIM, and one of the first steps is to convert the company from a normal limited company to a public limited company, or plc. This is a specific type of legal entity and only plc companies are allowed to trade on the stock exchange. The board also appoints one of the Big 4 accounting firms (the largest ones in the world – Deloitte, Ernst & Young, KPMG and PricewaterhouseCoopers) to be their auditors. They need top advisors to complete the Admission Document.

It is a big task. The auditors have to sign off the last three years of accounts, and the lawyers take the board members through the verification process. Because AIM is a public market, in effect the company has to conduct due diligence on itself. Every statement in the Admission Document has to be verified.

The nomad and lawyers go through the document line by line, asking for evidence to support every single statement that it makes. It is an arduous process, but the company makes it through. The Admission Document is signed off by the nomad and submitted to the AIM team at the London Stock Exchange. ABC is ready to be listed.

The nomad also acts as the company's stockbroker and arranges a roadshow for Annabel, Brian, Charlie and the new chairman to pitch the business to nearly forty institutional investors who are focused on AIM companies. Over a period of three weeks, they give three or four pitches every day, but it is entirely different to giving the VC or PE pitches they have done before. The stockbroker has already teed up the investor and sent them the Admission Document, so these pitches rarely last more than half an hour and are really a case of the investors getting a feel for the people behind the business. The investors could rely on everything in the Admission Document because it has been verified and approved.

When the roadshow is complete, ABC plc ends up with backing from a dozen institutional investors. Two of them take stakes of over 10% in the company, a few others take around 5% and the rest take smaller stakes. It is enough to buy out the angel network (although Nigel keeps a few shares) and the VC firm's shares. Annabel, Brian and Charlie are also able to sell some shares and take a little bit of cash off the table, but the three founders know they have to keep the rest of their shares for at least two years before they can sell.

The ABC story gives you a complete overview of the different types of equity funding available to companies as they grow, and some of the changes and challenges you may be faced with as the company develops.

Chapter wrap

In this chapter, the longest in the book by some measure, we've covered a great deal, including:

- Making sure the business is set up as a limited company

- Seeking professional advice; do not try to do this on your own

- The lesson from my dad to the fourteen-year-old me: what you borrow, you must pay back

- Seeking equity funding from different places as the business grows – pick appropriately

- Corporate governance

- Keeping your lenders and your investors informed

More than anything else, the thing I want you to take away from this chapter is to think in terms of abundance, not scarcity. There is more money out there than you can possibly imagine.

6

A Is For Acquire

'It is far better to buy a wonderful company at a fair price than a fair company at a wonderful price.'
— Warren Buffett

Once you have raised funds, it's time to start spending them. Depending on what is in your plan, you may buy some assets or hire a new team of people, but as an entrepreneur running a successful business, I'm sure you'll already know how to do that. For the purposes of this book, we'll focus on acquiring another business.

During my career I have bought companies ranging in price from £350,000 to £25 million. I have acquired another company that was listed on the London Stock Exchange, complying with the rules set out by the

Takeover Panel. I have experienced acquisitions that were wildly successful and others that were very challenging. Every deal has its own story and no two stories are the same, but there are a few common themes.

My first adult experience of the world of mergers and acquisitions came in the early 1990s when I was the Financial Controller of NCR Switzerland and our parent company, NCR Corporation, was taken over by the US telecoms giant, AT&T. I was not involved in the deal itself, but I certainly experienced first hand what it was like to be on the receiving end of a hostile takeover. That deal went on to become one of the worst ever corporate transactions, with billions of dollars of shareholder value destroyed before AT&T finally divested itself of NCR and re-floated the company on the New York Stock Exchange. I learned some early lessons on how not to do a deal, which I'll tell you more about in the next chapter, C is for Consolidate.

There are several books which tell you how to buy companies without using any of your (or your investors') money. That's one part of the market, but it's not what I'm talking about. As we have already seen in 'F Is For Fund', there is plenty of money available to be invested in the right business with the right leadership.

Cigar-butt investing

I'm a huge fan of Warren Buffett, one of the world's richest men and the only multi-billionaire who gained his fortune because of investing. Buffett talks about the early days of his career when he focused on what was cheap; he refers to it as 'cigar-butt investing'. You find a cigar butt on the pavement and pick it up. Sure you might get a few puffs and it won't have cost you anything, but it was someone else's cigar and they threw it away. You're getting the taste of their lips and mouth, their germs and whatever they didn't want any more.

I'm not saying it's always the wrong approach to take, but I don't want you to be constrained by looking only at what's cheap because of limited resources. If you've read this far, I'm assuming you must be comfortable with the idea of raising capital. Do that and you've got the money you need to build the business.

Warren Buffett is a patient man. He takes the time to identify companies that fit with his criteria. Companies that show long-term performance, have good growth potential and strong barriers to entry. Companies that he understands (which is why he completely side-stepped the dotcom boom, despite being described at the height of the boom as a dinosaur). Once he finds such a company, he decides what he believes the company is worth, and then he waits.

Many of his investments are in public companies, so every day the stock market gives him a price. Some days the price is above what Buffett thinks the company is worth. Sometimes he waits a long time, until one day, for whatever reason, the market decides the company is worth less than it was before, and less than Buffett thinks it is worth. As long as there hasn't been a fundamental change to the business, then Buffett acts, and he acts quickly and in large measure – often acquiring 5% or more of a public company, and almost always seeking to acquire as much as he can get his hands on. When dealing with privately held businesses, Buffett prefers to acquire 100% of the company.

Also, Buffett doesn't sell. He has often said that his preferred holding period is forever. He eschews cigar-butt opportunities, waiting until he is presented with an attractive opportunity to buy something he likes. He then takes swift action to acquire the business and stays with it for the long haul.

It's an approach that may seem foreign in the world of investing, and it is. It's also immensely successful. At the time of writing, Warren Buffett is the third richest person in the world with a net worth of $87 billion, so he's clearly doing something right.

Traditional steps to acquisition

There is a fairly well-trodden path to buying a company, which usually covers these steps:

- Initial contact between buyer and seller
- Agreeing heads of terms
- Due diligence
- Negotiating the sale and purchase agreement
- Completion
- Post-completion matters

Initial contact can happen in many ways. You could identify the company you want to buy and approach its board, or perhaps the seller will see you as the perfect partner to sell their company to and approach you. Often the deal is done through a business broker or a specialist corporate finance house that deals with buying and selling companies.

Although this is a corporate transaction we're talking about, in terms of your mindset, think of this as just another business dealing you have with an important supplier or customer. One party has something to sell and the other party wants to buy something. This initial contact will likely happen over a series of meetings and phone calls. You want to suss out and make sure you are comfortable with the other party – both the owner and the business. Think of it like going on a first date. You meet. You flirt. You decide whether you want to go on another one, or not.

I've seen this initial contact take place over drinks in a bar, over lunch or dinner, on the golf course, and in many other places. Sometimes the process happens quickly, and other times it takes a while. In one acquisition by Huveaux, the headline terms of the deal were agreed in one meeting. The principals met for a drink and quickly came to see the sense of a deal on both sides, so they celebrated with a bottle of champagne.

Alternatively, one of the acquisitions I completed took more than a year to get beyond the initial contact stage. It was a business my colleagues and I really wanted to acquire, but before selling, the founder wanted to be really sure. It was his baby and he wouldn't be rushed.

One missed acquisition was a company I wanted to buy but the owners refused to sell. Sometimes that happens. It's about building a relationship, after all. Don't rush it. Be patient, like Warren Buffett.

Heads of terms

Let's assume the first step has concluded well, and both parties agree that some kind of deal makes sense. At this stage you would start by setting out the high-level terms of the deal in a document referred to as 'heads of terms'. This would describe both parties and what they have been discussing as the structure of a deal. It would typically set out the expected purchase price and terms of settling that.

It should also include an exclusivity period, which prohibits the seller from discussing the business with other parties, and confidentiality provisions as you're going to get under the skin of the seller's business. This is important because you are about to start spending some serious money in the next stage, so this is the stage to bring your solicitors into the discussion. Heads of terms is a legal document and it needs to be drawn up properly by a lawyer or someone who has a lot of experience in doing deals to ensure you are properly protected.

It shouldn't be too long, though. It's the heads of terms, not the whole deal. There will be time to get into all the details later, and you haven't even started due diligence so don't have the full picture yet. To my mind, two or three pages is ideal for heads of terms. Anything more than five pages is getting excessive. Keep it simple and focused.

BUYING ASSETS OR SHARES?

The heads of terms would also set out whether you are acquiring the shares or the trade and assets of another company. We'll explore each of them in a little detail.

When you buy the shares of another company, you take on the ownership of that company, warts and all. The vendors will sell you their shares and now it is yours. If there are any historical issues – skeletons in the closet, one might say – they are now your responsibility. It might be that there's an old lawsuit lingering; perhaps it was threatened but then no action was taken, but all of a sudden the plaintiff sees there is a new owner and decides to raise the lawsuit again. Maybe there was a dispute with a former employee who was unfairly dismissed and is raising a case with the employment tribunal. Perhaps there is a change in some tax law that means the previously agreed tax returns are no longer valid and the tax man is coming after the company to claim the back taxes, plus interest and maybe even penalties. You bought the company – it's your problem.

On the other hand, there are upsides to buying the shares. You acquire everything – employees, contracts, leases, business names, the brand and other intellectual property, systems and processes. All of the assets are owned by the company and the ownership stays with the company. You won't need to change the title to assets, but do watch out for 'change in control' clauses in legal agreements like supplier and customer contracts.

When you buy the trade and assets, you are buying specific, identified things that will be carefully set out in the sale and purchase agreement. The upside is that you are not acquiring any of the company's history. You can in effect cherry pick the assets that you want and leave the rest behind for the owner of the company to deal with.

This route works well when you only want to acquire a certain part of a company, say the transport division of a logistics firm. You don't want the warehousing or the import/export department, you just want the firm's fleet of trucks and drivers. In this case, an asset deal makes sense.

Generally speaking, for the buyer it's more attractive to acquire the trade and assets, whereas for the seller it's more attractive to dispose of the whole company by way of shares sale, but if there's one thing I have learned in my years of doing deals, it's that every deal is different and you must look at each one individually. Whichever option you agree on, that forms the basis of the deal.

Time to spend some money

Once you have signed heads of terms and secured the exclusivity period, it's time for you to spend some money in the due diligence stage. This is where you and your team, along with your solicitors and accountants, crawl all over the target company.

Typically there are three areas to look into: legal, financial and commercial. You want to make sure that, from the discussions you and the vendors had, everything stacks up. On the legal side, if they told you they had fifty contracts with major clients, you'll want to see those contracts and know they really exist. Your solicitors will go through them in detail to ensure there are no problems or concerns with them. Same thing with employment contracts, supplier contracts, lease agreements, debt facilities and everything else.

On the financial side, your accountants will do a detailed review of the monthly financial statements of the target company to identify any seasonality issues, consistency of financial reporting, and review of tax returns and correspondence with tax authorities. They'll look at cash flow, debtors and creditors, and really get into the details behind the financial statements.

On the commercial side, you can use your external advisors, but in many cases this is where you and your management team come to the fore. You know the industry, the competitive landscape and the commercial issues that the target company is facing.

This stage is expensive because you're using external resources as well as your most senior people, but it's critical to ensure that you know what you're buying – *caveat emptor*.

Once you've finished the due diligence process, you'll need to sit down with your team and advisors to identify what you've all found. In my experience, there are always a few things that come up in the due diligence process. Sometimes more than a few. It's then a case of deciding how serious they are. Are there any findings that could constitute a deal breaker?

In one deal I did, several material issues came up in due diligence that might have been deal breakers. In the end we negotiated a 15% reduction in the purchase price we'd agreed at heads of terms – the reduction saved us more than a million pounds.

Many things can come to light. For example, the fifty contracts with major clients you had been told about don't really exist; they are just verbal arrangements that have been maintained over many years on a 'gentlemen's agreement'. Perhaps there is a dispute with the tax authorities over some past taxes. Or it might be that none of the findings on their own constitutes a serious concern, but so many little things came out of due diligence that you no longer feel comfortable.

In my experience, the fewer the surprises, the better. If you and the vendor have established a good rapport in the early discussions and you are both serious about doing a deal, then as the negotiations progress, the vendor should be telling you a little more in each discussion. By the time it gets to heads of terms, you want to have a pretty good idea of what's going on in the target company. There's no excuse for not doing due diligence, but you don't want to be finding any major surprises during the process. What would that tell you about the honesty of the people you are dealing with?

Sale and purchase agreement

Once the due diligence process is finished, it's time to get down to negotiating and drafting the sale and purchase agreement (SPA). This is the legal document that sets out all of the terms of the deal. You need experienced solicitors to take the lead on this. Please do not try to do it yourself.

Depending on the complexity of the deal, the SPA will typically run anywhere from twenty-five to several hundred pages. For the majority of acquisitions I've done, it's usually been in the range of thirty to fifty pages.

The SPA will generally cover:

- Parties to the agreement – as with any legal document, it's important to set out clearly the names and other details of the legal entities and / or people being bound into the agreement. At the cleanest level there is one buyer and one seller, but there can be complex deals with multiple buyers and sellers, and it is important that there is no doubt as to who is who. It's not uncommon to see one buyer and many sellers where the target company has multiple shareholders. In this case, each selling shareholder must be a party to the agreement.

- Agreement between the parties to sell and to purchase – it may sound obvious, but this step is of critical importance. This is where each party states that it agrees to do what is set out in the document that follows. Do not skip it.

- The purchase price, which is often referred to as consideration – this sets out how the shares or assets are going to be paid for, which may be a combination of cash at completion, deferred cash payment to be made at a future date subject to certain conditions being met, shares in the acquiring company, and debt in the form of loan notes issued by the buyer to the seller.

- For deals with service-based companies, where it's all about the relationship, it's not uncommon to see the sellers tied into the new company for a period of two to four years to ensure a complete handover of the relationships. A big chunk of the consideration will be deferred until the end of that time, which is commonly referred to as an earn-out.

- Representations and warranties – these are the legal terms for promises made and things that are guaranteed, respectively. This is where things that came up in due diligence are set out, so that the parties are all in clear understanding and agreement. Additionally, the sellers will make representations that they are in fact the owners of the shares they are about to sell and that the company has the power to enter into the transaction, and there will be many more. The representations and warranties are often set out in schedules at the back of the SPA, but do not think that makes them any less important. This is the first place you go when something has gone wrong.

- Indemnities – if the representations and warranties given turn out to be untrue, the indemnity section will set out the remedies in case the buyer suffers loss or damages. There is usually an agreed mechanism for making claims under the indemnities, and as part of the agreement they are legally binding on all parties. Enforcement may still be difficult, and I've had experience of disputed indemnity claims that went to arbitration before being settled, but this is the place where the rules are set out.

- Restrictive covenants – these are things the sellers are restricted from doing once the deal is done, with a view to protecting the buyer's ongoing interest in the business. Typically the covenants will include things like restricting the sellers from starting, joining or investing in a competing business for a number of years after the deal or enticing away employees, customers and suppliers of the company. They are restrictive, but must not be onerous or they may not stand up to challenge in court.

- Completion matters – this sets out the exact things that need to happen for the deal to complete and title in the shares or assets to transfer. They will include things like delivery of the original share certificates and the statutory books and records of the company, and payment of the purchase consideration (at least the amount due at completion – remember some may be deferred).

- Post-completion matters – this sets out the rules for things that happen after completion, for instance the settlement of any deferred consideration and the process for making indemnity claims.

Disclosure letter

In addition to the SPA, typically the seller(s) will prepare a disclosure letter which is usually delivered a day or two prior to completion. This is an important document because it discloses any specific issues that would otherwise represent a breach of the representations and warranties.

For example, there could be a warranty that the company has no open disputes with the tax authorities. If it subsequently comes to light that there was a dispute in a particular year, unless it was disclosed, it could give rise to an indemnity claim. Another example might be that no customer represents more than 5% of total sales revenue, but in actual fact one customer has 7%. Disclosure gives the buyer the full picture.

The basic premise here is that the representations and warranties are written as all-encompassing statements, and then anything that goes against those statements is disclosed. At this stage, the buyer still has the right to walk away from the deal if the risk of the disclosed item is too high, but most of the time any material matters will have already come up in the due diligence stage.

Post-completion, the SPA continues to be an important document, as anything that arises after the deal has been completed will be regulated and settled in accordance with its terms.

Walking away

Finally, let's look at walking away from a deal. It's hard, but sometimes necessary.

At each step, from initial contact through to the instant before completion, as the buyer, you have the ability to walk away from the deal. As you progress through the steps, the seller(s) should be sharing more and more information with you. In fact, insist on this. At some point, the information may put up enough red flags that you decide the deal is no longer attractive. Or perhaps something happens in your business that means you can't complete the deal.

The key thing to understand is that until completion, it's not too late, although as the deal progresses, it gets harder. People sometimes refer to 'deal fever' when the desire to complete the deal gets in the way of making what might be the sensible decision to walk away.

I've experienced deals that got to the end of due diligence, and then the buyer decided the risks the process identified were too great. It's painful to walk away when you've got the sunk costs of everything you've done so far towards the deal, but it's better than ending up with a bad deal.

Chapter wrap

In this chapter we've covered:

- The traditional steps that lead to an acquisition
- The distinction between buying assets and buying shares
- The most important document: the SPA

More than anything else, the thing I want you to take away from this chapter is the quote from Warren Buffett:

'It is far better to buy a wonderful company at a fair price than a fair company at a wonderful price.'

7

C Is For Consolidate

'When you run an entrepreneurial business, you have hurry sickness – you don't look back, you advance and consolidate. But it is such fun.'
— Anita Roddick

While Fund and Acquire may be considered the sexy parts of the FACE methodology, Consolidate is where the hard work begins. It is also the area that decides whether the acquisition is a successful one or not. This is where you put two companies together, and at least one of them is going to face a significant change in values and culture.

One of the titans of the UK's mergers and acquisitions (M&A) scene in the latter half of the 20th century was Lord Hanson of conglomerate Hanson plc. Word has it, the first thing that happened after completion of an acquisition by Hanson was that the facilities boss would pay a visit to the chief executive of the acquired company and remove whatever office furniture he or she had. This was immediately replaced by the standard issue furniture for the leader of a Hanson group subsidiary. It was high-quality furniture, no doubt, but more importantly, it sent a strong signal to the newly acquired business and its leader: we are now the owners of this business and you must play by our rules. It was a clear sign of the culture change that was about to come.

The challenges of changing culture

My first adult exposure to the world of mergers and acquisitions, and to experiencing the Consolidate stage, came in the early 1990s when I was the Financial Controller of NCR Switzerland, and AT&T completed a hostile takeover bid for NCR Corporation, our parent company. When the deal was completed, the company was renamed AT&T Global Information Solutions and rebranded to align with the AT&T branding. That was natural and to be expected, but what came next was the interesting part.

NCR's culture had been command and control. There was a clear hierarchy and we all knew our place within the organisation. In the finance department, NCR's global finance and accounting policy manual set out the rules of everything that we had to do and how to do it. I remember there being five or six lever-arch files (ring binders if you're reading this in North America) and we had to follow those rules.

AT&T seemed to be much more relaxed about this. The company had its own policy manuals, but they were far less detailed, and the overriding difference I remember was that at AT&T there was more of a sense of trust and shared accountability. Command and control meets trust and shared accountability. It was an interesting juxtaposition of values and culture.

In 1993 I moved from Switzerland to the UK as the financial controller of the newly named AT&T Global Information Solutions UK. The powers that be selected me along with a dozen or so others from around the organisation and we were charged with rolling out a new management approach based around coaching people rather than command and control. It sat well with me because I've always rebelled against strict command and control, but it was fascinating to observe the impact it had on certain people in the company.

Old titles like manager and director were eliminated. The group CEO announced that he was to be known as the Head Coach, and anyone who had been a manager of people became a coach. Subordinates were called associates. Everyone in the company was a coach or an associate, and in many cases, for the layers between the Head Coach and entry level, staff were both a coach to the people below them and an associate to those above. That bit was confusing.

The small group that I was now part of was sent away for training on what it meant to behave like a coach. It was a train-the-trainer type programme. Many people loved the new programme and the concept that they were more empowered than ever before. Several of the senior people in the company embraced coaching, but for a few of the longer-serving people who had climbed the greasy pole to become heads of department or division in the command and control culture, it didn't sit well with them at all.

AT&T's acquisition of NCR turned out to be one of the worst M&A transactions in corporate history, certainly until some of the dotcom takeover deals. It's funny because on so many levels it should have succeeded.

I remember the front cover of AT&T's annual report a couple of years after the deal had gone through. AT&T had recently acquired one of the leading mobile phone businesses in North America and it was all about the integration between computing and telecommunications. The front cover featured a young person on a skateboard holding a mobile phone with the words 'Any time, anywhere, any device'. Although AT&T was strategically bang on the money, the deal was at least ten years ahead of its time, and the combination of the two cultures was doomed. It was a fabulous learning experience for me, and one that you can benefit from too.

Moving away from the giga-sized global corporate deals, it's also interesting to consider what happens to the former owners of a company once the deal completes. In acquisitions of PR agencies, the founders were always tied in for an earn-out period because it was a relationship business. The acquiring company focused on taking over those relationships before the expiry of the earn-out, which is often the case in service businesses where it's all about relationships.

With product-based businesses it is often the opposite, and that was certainly the case for the acquisitions at Huveaux. With few exceptions, the owners of the business left the company at the time of acquisition. We were, however, keen to keep on the management just below owner/MD level, and we were at great pains to bring them into our values and culture.

This is the stage when the new owner is most at risk. Get things wrong and the key employees, customers and suppliers can disappear quickly. Sometimes the changes are minimal, but one of the key reasons for buying another company is to bring it into your way of doing business. It's a fast way to get more customers, more suppliers and more skilled staff. You can also integrate brands and take on more sophisticated systems and processes from acquired businesses, as we did at Huveaux. Equally, sometimes you need to take tough decisions and make some cuts.

Restructuring for growth

One of the first consolidate jobs I was responsible for came in 2000, when I was working as European CFO of BSMG, an acquisitive PR agency based out of New York that was owned by a second-tier advertising agency. It was another job that I got because of my language skills. BSMG had recently expanded into Europe and had acquired two PR agencies in Germany – one in Hamburg and the other in Munich.

Head office in New York wasn't getting any information or financials from the businesses in Germany. They weren't cooperating. Shortly after joining BSMG, I was spending two or three days a week in the Hamburg and Munich offices, getting to know the people and getting them to open up and share information with me so I could feed it back to New York.

Not long after that, BSMG decided to merge the two legal entities into one, and the chap who ran the Munich office became the CEO of the business in Germany. We restructured the business, moving all of the finance and administration functions to Munich, and I recruited a new financial controller – someone I would recruit again into another business in 2006. Hamburg continued as the office looking after clients in northern Germany, but the drive behind the growth in Germany was in Munich.

We later took on a team of people who had built up a small PR agency servicing clients who were listing on the then-booming junior market of the Frankfurt Stock Exchange, the Neuer Markt. Because of the structure we had set up, we were able to simply take them on as new employees and drop their entire client billing and management activities into the systems and processes we had built in Munich.

It ran smoothly. I remember at the end of the year getting a handwritten note from the global CEO of BSMG thanking me for sorting out the mess and helping turn Germany into a real powerhouse for growth in the group.

The tough side – making cuts

When Huveaux bought Parliamentary Communications, I was given the job of restructuring the operations in the newly acquired Brussels office. Unlike the UK operations of the new business, which were profitable, the Brussels office was suffering significant losses.

The day after completion, I was on the first Eurostar to Brussels in the morning. When I arrived there were fifteen staff in the office. When I left that evening there were just four. This was a challenge on two fronts: telling eleven people in one day that they no longer have a job is not easy, but more importantly, I had to gather the remaining four staff members together and get them on board. They were faced with the shock of losing most of their colleagues, and in many cases were wondering why it was they who still had a job when many others did not.

Fortunately, because I had personal experience of my employer being acquired and my role being made redundant, as well as experience of being the acquirer wielding the bad news, I was able to reassure the small team about their roles and explain why I had taken the action I did. In situations like this, it can really help to share your own vulnerability to gain the trust of others. It was a hard day, and coming back on Eurostar that evening, I had more than a couple of gin and tonics to calm the nerves down.

It was serious business, but there was a little dark humour that came out of it. There is an underground newspaper in Brussels called *The Sprout*, and the former MD of the Brussels business posted an article lamenting the bloodshed at his company, referring to the fact that the first thing he did when I arrived was to buy me a coffee. And then I fired him.

After leaving Huveaux, I joined a company called GoIndustry plc, which had just completed its listing on AIM. GoIndustry was a dotcom survivor that was a blend of online and traditional bricks and mortar business auctioning surplus industrial equipment.

A little over a year after I joined the company, we found out that our largest global competitor, a company called DoveBid, was for sale by its private equity owners. In early 2008, we raised £18 million on the stock exchange and completed the acquisition. The subsequent consolidation was unquestionably the hardest and most complex of any of the acquisitions I have ever done. It turned into a two-year project and it nearly killed me.

Prior to the deal, GoIndustry operated in sixteen countries and DoveBid was in about a dozen. When we put the two companies together, we created the largest company in the field of auctioning surplus industrial machinery and equipment worldwide. When all was said and done with the consolidation, we operated in twenty-three countries around the world. The only significant overlaps were in the UK, the USA and Germany. There were a few smaller countries where both companies had a presence, but in those three, both companies were big.

One of the primary justifications for the deal, and the key message that we put across to the investors when raising the money to buy DoveBid, was that there was a big overlap in those three countries and we could rip out a significant amount of duplicate costs. The goal was to cut costs by £5 million, which was about 20% of the combined cost base of the two companies.

As CFO working with the finance leaders in each country, it was my job to track the achievements against the plan and to work with the country heads to ensure we implemented the plan. I also worked with our legal team to shut down duplicate legal entities in the countries where there was overlap. Finally, I was tasked with shutting down DoveBid's head office in Los Angeles. This consolidate project was a huge team effort and took nearly six months to execute after the acquisition was completed.

To rip out that level of cost, we had to focus our attention on one main area: people. My colleagues and I started by putting together lists of all staff and their roles in all locations around the world, and then we had to make the difficult decisions. Which roles would remain unchanged, which ones might be combined, and which ones were going to be eliminated?

Once we had done that, it was time to commence the consultation process as we were implementing redundancies around the world. Every country has its own employment laws and we had to ensure that everything we did in each country was in compliance. We did our best to be fair and equitable, and to treat those who lost their jobs with dignity and respect. It was a tough time, and 109 people lost their jobs from around the company, mainly in the UK, USA and Germany. We were able to save more than £4 million in costs from this exercise.

DoveBid's head office was the next to go, and that was my responsibility. We didn't need two executive teams and their various central support functions, but the big risk was the loss of institutional knowledge.

Over the course of a year, from the initial deal negotiations until we finally shut down DoveBid's head office, I made thirteen trips to Los Angeles. It was good for accumulating air miles! The reason for this was to ensure I could have enough time with the outgoing management team and their staff to know I had a good grasp of what was going on in the DoveBid business and to ensure we transitioned as much of the knowledge as possible. One of the great successes was that I managed to get one member of DoveBid's finance team to move from Los Angeles to Baltimore on the east coast where our North America head office was based. This was a critical step in helping to preserve institutional knowledge.

INSTITUTIONAL KNOWLEDGE

A great example of the loss of institutional knowledge was in 2001 when BSMG's parent company was taken over by Interpublic Group (IPG). BSMG was merged into IPG's Weber Shandwick PR business, which was probably twenty-five times the size of BSMG in Europe. My boss and I had completed seven acquisitions of PR agencies in the previous two years and we were both shown the door by the new owners. Weber Shandwick's European team would be responsible for the BSMG business.

About six months later I received the first phone call. Something had come up on one of the deals and nobody knew the back story, or how to address and resolve the issue. That was the first of quite a few pieces of consulting work I ended up doing for the new owners.

The best part came about a year after my position had been made redundant. IPG's auditors were trying to complete the audit of their financial statements and there were more than a few questions that nobody in Weber Shandwick was able to answer. That led to nearly three months of full-time consulting work for me.

Over the years I have seen so many cases of people leaving organisations through redundancy programmes, only to come back in the following weeks and months as consultants on much higher rates of pay than they were on as employees. Watch out for that when you're planning the Consolidate phase.

The rest of the savings from the GoIndustry-DoveBid consolidation came from a number of smaller initiatives across the group, and in the autumn of 2008 we went back to the stock exchange to announce that the acquisition was complete; that we had made the cost-savings; and that everything was on track as we had planned it.

A couple of weeks later, Lehman Brothers went bust and the global financial crisis was in full swing. We lost a huge amount of business we'd expected to have in the fourth quarter of 2008, and having just completed a global consolidation exercise, we found it hard to move quickly to adapt. The lost revenue fell straight to the bottom line. In 2009 we had to start the cost cutting all over again.

This time the goal was to remove £6 million of costs so that we could be profitable at a seriously reduced level of revenue compared with what we'd envisaged when we did the deal. This time it was really hard, because we had made all the cuts we'd planned from putting the two businesses together, but it was a question of survival, so we made the tough decisions and implemented more cuts. Everyone on the executive team took pay cuts and many more people lost their jobs. We examined every line item of expenditure to find potential savings, and a number of smaller country units were sold or shut down if we couldn't run them profitably.

The positive side – new opportunities

Consolidate doesn't always mean restructuring and cost cutting. There are plenty of examples of companies that have been bought because they offered a key missing element – that might be people, brands, systems and processes or something else – in the acquiring entity. Acquisition is often the fastest way of addressing and resolving that gap.

In 2017, one of my clients, a company that operates primarily in the UK and Australia, acquired several service businesses that it had been working with closely in the UK. It was now able to offer their services to its clients in Australia as well, whereas previously external parties had serviced the Australian clients.

At Huveaux, having presence in the political publishing markets in the UK, France and Brussels positioned us as the leading political publishing business in Europe and gave the company many opportunities to support and serve its customers.

Chapter wrap

In this chapter we've covered:

- The challenges of changing values and culture
- The tougher side of consolidation – cutting costs
- The positive side of consolidation – new opportunities

More than anything else, the thing I want you to take away from this chapter is that this is the human side of the game. Changing values and culture and cutting costs are all about people. So is the positive side: the new opportunities. Look out for people and you will get through this hardest part of the FACE methodology just fine.

8

E Is For Exit

'Affairs are easier of entrance than of exit; and it is but common prudence to see our way out before we venture in.'
— Aesop

In many respects, the Exit phase is pretty much the same as the Acquire phase, except that you're sitting on the other side of the transaction. In reality, as Aesop suggests, it is far more complex than that.

The emotional rollercoaster

The mantra here is prepare, prepare, prepare. Prepare your business so that you can maximise your exit valuation. If you've made acquisitions then you'll know what the process is all about. Prepare for due diligence, when the buyer sends in the lawyers and accountants who will crawl all over everything. Prepare yourself for an emotional rollercoaster, because you are on the verge of selling the business that you started or bought, and into which you have poured your heart and soul, and one day soon it's not going to be yours any more.

Some days you'll feel excited and elated. Other days you'll feel a sense of trepidation or fear. Still other days you'll be filled with worry about the people you are leaving behind – the staff, customers and suppliers with whom you have built relationships over many years. There will even be days when you cycle between all of the above, and maybe even more emotions. Follow the Scouts' motto: 'Be prepared'.

Routes to exit

There are multiple routes to a potential exit, and we'll take a look at each of the main ones:

- Liquidation
- Passing the business on to the next generation
- Trade sale
- Management buyout (MBO)
- Buy in management buyout (BIMBO)
- IPO on a stock exchange

Liquidation is the least attractive exit route, as it usually offers the lowest valuation, but sometimes it's the only route available. My father-in-law ran a general practitioner (GP) practice in Canada for many years, in a city that had a plethora of GP practices. When it came time for him to retire, there were no buyers for his business. The main proceeds came from selling the leasehold on the office where his practice was located.

Liquidation is often the case for so-called 'one man band' businesses, because in reality there is nothing to sell. When the owner leaves the business there is nothing left. If you find yourself in a liquidation situation, you have two choices: accept that you're only going to be able to sell the assets in the company, often at a fraction of their value, or take the time to create a business with other people so it's not entirely dependent on you. I'm going to make an informed assumption that if you've made it this far in the book, it's unlikely you have a business that is facing liquidation, but sometimes it happens.

Passing the business on to the next generation is how family businesses can continue, and sometimes thrive, but this can be fraught with difficulties. What if there are non-family shareholders? If you've followed the FACE methodology, this could well be the case. Is there a family member who is ready, willing and able to take the business over? If there is, to what degree are you willing to cede control to the next generation?

Stories abound of family businesses where the second or third generation are involved in the day-to-day, but the important strategic decisions are taken by the elderly matriarch or patriarch of the family who won't relinquish power.

I remember pitching to a family business a few years back where the eldest son was notionally in charge of what went on, but his father, who was in his eighties, wouldn't allow him to make any changes to the business: things like investing in a website and building a social media presence. The ironic thing is that this company had the word 'progressive' in its name. I also remember pitching in the early noughties to two sisters who ran a travel agency that was struggling, and they were waiting for the day that 'this internet thing goes away'.

Family businesses can become increasingly challenging with each passing from one generation to the next. This is not just because different egos get involved, but the shareholding invariably becomes more widely distributed and there might be marriages and divorces which only add to the complexity. Don't get me wrong, there are many successful family businesses, and some of them (like the fund-management company Fidelity or household-products company SC Johnson) have grown into global leaders in their industry, but it's not always plain sailing.

Trade sale is where you sell the company to another company, often a competitor or a new entrant in the market. This is probably the most common exit route for entrepreneurial businesses, but that doesn't mean it is easy. It really depends on the business and the market you are operating in.

A growing, profitable company in a stable or expanding industry is much more attractive than a small, loss-making business in a stagnating or declining industry. I'll refer you back to the opening mantra of this chapter: prepare, prepare, prepare. If you're thinking about trade sale, then start grooming your business now to make it attractive to potential buyers.

I've come across many entrepreneurs who started a company in their twenties and never really thought about where it was going or what they wanted to do when it was time for them to move on. Many ended up building what is referred to as a 'lifestyle business' that allows the owner to carry on their lifestyle – which may or may not be an affluent one – and run their business for many years without ever creating any value for themselves. If you want to know more about this, check out Appendix 3 – Valuation.

A TRADE SALE

A few years ago, the founders of a company I had worked with decided to sell the business. Unlike previous cases I have shared that were public companies listed on the stock market, this one was a private company that sold to another private company. I'm not at liberty to name the company, the individuals involved or disclose amounts, so we'll call the company XYZ Limited.

There were three founding partners who each had equal ownership of the company, although one of them left after a few years. His stake was bought by the other two. We launched the business and grew it organically over several years, reaching a peak of several million in revenues and more than twenty employees.

XYZ continued to operate successfully at this level, but there were tensions between the partners, and eventually the board decided that the best way to secure the future of the company and the value that the founders had built up in it was to sell.

Through our collective networks, we identified several parties who might be interested in acquiring the company. After a number of meetings and discussions, we narrowed it down to two potential buyers who were a good cultural fit with XYZ. We then solicited offers from both and one was the clear winner.

Once we had agreed heads of terms, the board asked me to lead the exit process so that the founders could continue to focus their time and attention on maintaining the business. At the conclusion of the due diligence process, I was delighted when the CFO of the buyer told me that ours was the cleanest due diligence he had experienced.

With due diligence out of the way, it was time to negotiate the SPA. Because of my experience with acquisitions at BSMG, Huveaux and GoIndustry, I was able to structure the deal in a way that resulted in an incremental 15% being added to the buyer's original offer. It was a multi-million pound exit.

The founders were engaged by the new owners to assist with the transition and had two-year employment contracts with an earn-out. One of them left at the expiry of the earn-out period, while the other decided to stay on and ran a division of the buyer's business, a position he held for several years before moving on.

This is a good example of an exit where everybody wins. The founders received their payments in accordance with the terms of the deal. The buyer acquired a business with experienced people and a recognised brand and merged it into its existing operation, which was significantly strengthened by the deal. After the expiry of their earn-out period and other restrictive covenants, both founders moved on to other things in their personal careers.

The next two routes to exit are MBO and BIMBO. This is where the owner sells to the existing management team, or sells to someone who buys in and joins the management team to ultimately lead the MBO, like Jeremy, the new CEO who joined ABC when it raised funds from the PE house to buy out Nigel's angel network and the VC firm.

The advantage of this type of deal is that the due diligence process during the Acquisition phase and the whole of the Consolidation phase are much cleaner, because everyone knows what is going on inside the company. This is also a great way to secure and retain the services of key staff, if they know there will be an opportunity for them to take over the ownership of the business.

At the time of writing, I'm working with a successful hair and beauty company where the owner of thirty-five years is selling to several members of her team who have been running the day-to-day operations. She is moving on to start another company and will use her proceeds from the deal to finance the startup and early growth costs of the new business.

The main challenge of the MBO route is ensuring there are people in your team who are willing and able to take over the business. Owning and running a company is not everyone's cup of tea, and it's a big change from being part of the team to being the owner. If you're thinking about doing an exit by MBO, it's important that you help your staff to gain the skills and experience they will need to run the company successfully.

PE buyers will often become involved at the MBO/BIMBO stage, particularly when the management team lacks the financial resources to complete the transaction. It is not uncommon for PE houses to back a management team.

GOING FULL CIRCLE

A great example of a successful MBO backed by PE is that of my friend Alain Trébucq. Remember the best deal I ever did? The acquisition of ATP Egora by Huveaux? Well, ATP stands for Alain Trébucq Publishing.

Alain sold his business to France Telecom in 2001. France Telecom merged it with its medical publishing site www.egora.fr to form ATP Egora, which Huveaux bought. Huveaux then bought JBB Santé and combined the two businesses to form its medical division. A couple of years after I left, Alain agreed a deal with the board of Huveaux to buy the medical publishing business. It was in effect an exit going full circle: Alain sold his business to France Telecom, which merged it with another business and then sold it to Huveaux, which merged it with another business and then sold it back to Alain. To add a twist to the going full circle tale, when Alain left medical practice in the 1980s to start his career as a medical journalist, his first employer was JBB Santé!

Alain has been at the helm of each transaction and has seen the company grow and change. He has encountered many challenges along the way: the dotcom crash, the 2008 financial crisis, and more recently a severe drop in revenue from advertising, yet he has adapted to them all and continues to run a successful business to this day.

I recently sat down with Alain to discuss the role of passion in work, how to overcome difficulty and the importance of keeping your eyes on the cash. When I asked him why he decided to buy back what his own business had evolved into, he answered, 'Circumstances.'

Alain was the general manager of Huveaux's French subsidiary from 2006. In January 2008, the CEO of Huveaux told him that the board wished to sell the French medical division. This business formed around 90% of the total activity of Huveaux France, but Huveaux only wanted to keep the political publishing business, Le Trombinoscope. Alain thought it was a real opportunity to run his own business again, by going through an MBO with a PE house backing him.

The deal completed in June 2008, a few months before the financial crisis hit. Supported by the French PE firm EPF, Alain invested just over €1 million of his own money for a 51% stake in the company; EPF invested just under €1 million in return for 47%; and Alain's CFO bought the remaining 2%. EPF also invested €2 million by way of convertible loan notes and secured a debt facility of €6.5 million. (See Appendix 2 for further details of how PE deals are financed.)

Since the financial crisis, the medical industry in France has been under tremendous political pressure. As with most countries that have state-funded healthcare, the French government has been at pains to keep the cost of drugs under control. Pharma revenues in France have been flat for the past ten years, which has put huge burdens on drug company advertising budgets.

When Huveaux bought JBB Santé in 2005, advertising represented nearly 100% of its revenue, but Huveaux knew the model was changing. Today advertising is just 30%, with another 40% coming from subscriptions and the remaining 30% from CPD. Total revenues have declined, but Alain believes the risk profile of the business is significantly lower. Instead of nearly 100% of revenues being dependent on the advertising budgets of twenty to thirty major pharmaceutical companies, today 70% of revenues come from 30,000 doctors throughout France.

The combination of the digital transformation of the publishing industry and changing trends in medical advertising has been difficult to contend with, but Alain is still running the business at a profitable margin and has managed the change in structure well. His advice from this experience?

'Do not take your eyes off your cash. In the medical press, we were used to big advertising revenues and no cash problems. I must admit that for years, I managed the company without a close eye on cash. Since buying the company in 2008, we have lost 70% of our advertising revenues, and if we do better than just survive, it is because we have managed to change our business model. There is now little that is advertising-dependent, and we keep our eyes on cash every day.'

And in terms of what it takes to run a successful business? Alain sums it up in one word: passion. A passionate entrepreneur communicates his enthusiasm to his teams and his customers while protecting himself, including against burnout. When passion disappears, it's time to turn the page.

It's safe to say that Alain has had an incredible journey, and it looks likely to keep going. In 2008 he made a ten-year deal with the French PE firm to buy Huveaux's medical division. Today it is the last investment in the fund EPF raised. Perhaps there is an opportunity for a deal to buy out EPF and take over the rest of the company with his current management team?

Considering his exciting career, I asked Alain what his favourite part of running a business is.

'Freedom of enterprise by focusing on the medium and long term.'

IPO

The final route to exit is the IPO, which is when you float your company on a stock exchange. London's AIM is one such route for smaller companies coming to the stock exchange for the first time, and NASDAQ Stockholm has also risen in prominence in recent years for European businesses looking to do an IPO. Most countries have an arm of their main stock market for smaller companies, but both AIM and NASDAQ Stockholm welcome companies from anywhere in the world.

IPO can be an extremely profitable exit route, especially if the share price rises after the company goes public. On the other hand, there is a risk that the shares can bomb. It's not for the faint-hearted.

Additionally, to be successful with an IPO exit, you must have grown the business to a size where it can bear the costs of listing and the ongoing compliance of being a publicly traded company. It can easily cost half a million pounds in fees to list a company on a market like AIM, and potentially much more if you list on the main market. Ongoing costs can run into the hundreds of thousands every year for various advisors, auditors, non-executive directors and other compliance costs, so it's clearly not for everybody.

Often in an IPO, the founder of a business faces a restricted period when they are not allowed to sell any of their shares. This is designed to allow the establishment of an orderly market in the shares and enable a base of institutional and other investors to pick up the stock. It is not uncommon to see a founder sell a portion (up to a quarter or possibly a third) of their holding at IPO to take some money off the table, but the remaining holding may be locked in for a few years.

Unlike the other exit routes, IPO doesn't have to see you leave the business. It simply gives you the vehicle via the stock market to enable you to sell some or all of your shares. There are many cases of entrepreneurs who have listed their companies on the stock market and carried on running them for many years. Being listed gives you access to a significant pool of cash should you wish to raise more money for the company. Perhaps that is a circular route you can follow to start the FACE methodology all over again.

Chapter wrap

In this chapter we've covered:

- The emotional rollercoaster you'll be facing

- Routes to a potential exit

- The possibility of going full circle

More than anything else, the thing I want you to take away from this chapter is to be prepared. This applies to every step of the FACE methodology, but Exit is all about the final realisation of your dreams and you don't want to fall at the last hurdle, as the saying goes.

9

Case Study: New Generation

New Generation is a UK-focused agent and whole-saler, importing a range of quality wines, champagnes and spirits from around the world. It supplies hotels, restaurants, cafés and retail wine merchants. I met founder James Booth in 2010 when I launched my wine business and am still a customer of New Generation today.

Although he didn't know it at the time, when I first met him, James had already implemented the first three steps in the FACE methodology:

- He had **F**unded the business, seeking external investors to support growth.

- He had **A**cquired several businesses.

- He had Consolidated them well. As James told me, 'The vendors needed a solution. With a friendly team and my experience in corporate finance, we've been able to complete on deals that have let us keep the key people in the business.'

When I first approached James about being in the book, he responded by saying, 'You'll have to change your methodology from FACE to FAC, because I'm having far too much fun building a business in an industry that I love to even contemplate Exit.' Undaunted by his cheeky retort, I decided to continue because this is an interesting story of successful growth by acquisition in an industry whose product is near and dear to my heart – not to mention my palate.

With a degree in French and Business, and an early career in the City working for several well-established merchant banks, James tells the story of how he ended up in the wine trade.

'On my year abroad at university, I did a wine exchange in Burgundy. Friends of my family have their own estate in Chablis, and since I was doing a degree in French it made sense to live and work there. I spent a whole season working in the vineyards and the winery. It was fascinating.'

Returning to the UK, James worked for eight years in investment banking, but it wasn't his calling. The prospect of flogging derivatives for the rest of his life was looking less and less appealing, and eventually the call of the wine trade won. During this time he started a private wine club called Grape Juice for some friends in the City. James had his vision. He knew what he wanted to do.

Wise acquisitions

In 2005, James launched New Generation Wines, teaming up with a City contact who became one of his financial backers and is still a partner in the business today. Rather than starting from scratch, James and his business partner set up a holding company and bought a small wine merchant called Ford Record Wines. James also rolled Grape Juice into the mix, and they changed the name of the company to New Generation Wines.

Buying an established business is a clever move for an entrepreneur looking to make a fast foothold in a market. Rather than starting with nothing and building it all from scratch, acquiring an existing company means that you have customers, suppliers, staff and a brand in the market from day one. You can build the business from there. It's a great alternative to bootstrapping.

James and the team worked hard to strengthen the relationship with Ford Record's agency supplier, France's Domaine Gayda, to ensure they could build the estate's presence in the UK market. In 2006, they brought in two senior executives, attracting them with the opportunity to buy shares in the company. This was a critical move, as the company needed skilled executives to drive its growth organically.

The contacts from Domaine Gayda later introduced James to the boutique South African producer Boekenhoutskloof that agreed a distribution deal with New Generation. In 2008 the owners of Boekenhoutskloof purchased an equity stake in New Generation. James used this to fund organic growth and strengthen the team further, bringing in another key executive who also bought shares in the company.

In 2010 James made New Generation's next acquisition, buying the trade and assets of Stokes Fine Wines. James knew the team at Stokes because they were customers, buying some of the wines New Generation imported from Boekenhoutskloof, which they sold on to a prestige London retailer. James met with the buyers at the retailer and asked why they were buying through a distributor rather than from the importer directly. This led to a discussion about the Stokes business, and James decided to approach the owners of Stokes with an offer to buy them out.

The company was in a bit of a state, with too much stock on the books and some issues in terms of controlling operations. The executives James had brought into New Generation and offered equity stakes to were experienced in the wine trade, and the company was able to sort these problems out.

Buying Stokes brought additional benefits. It gave James and his partners direct access to the prestige retailer's buyers and New Generation was able to offer its entire range to them. It also brought them additional suppliers and customers that Stokes had developed over the years. This was an acquisition of the assets owned by Stokes, as opposed to buying the shares of the company.

To fund the acquisition, New Generation used existing bank facilities. The deal was structured with deferred compensation payable to the vendors, based on the growth of the combined business and the ability to take on and sell the Stokes stock. It was a success, and with the added scale, New Generation started to make a mark, including winning Small Agent of the Year at the International Wine Challenge in 2012. That was a key achievement for the business and something New Generation would not have done on its own.

Where the old meets the new

In 2015, James got wind that a well-established wine and spirits business called McKinley Vintners was struggling. As he puts it, 'There was a lovely old galleon, a really beautiful boat, but she was leaking badly. We offered to fix her up.'

This was a transformational acquisition. As its name might suggest, New Generation was strongly focused on the 'new world' in wine terms. It had little representation of wineries from the 'old world', in particular Bordeaux, Burgundy and Champagne. New Generation had built an impressive customer list, but it was unable to serve those customers with wines from the biggest selling regions. McKinley Vintners also had spirits distribution, which was an entirely new area for New Generation.

McKinley was struggling because it had just lost two of its leading agency brands, champagne house Gosset and the cognac brand Frapin, both of which had recently been sold by the Cointreau family. This loss led, as James puts it, to the galleon being holed below the water. At the age of seventy, founder Peter McKinley was not up for rebuilding the business, and James acted quickly to buy him out.

They agreed the deal whereby New Generation acquired all of the shares in McKinley Vintners Limited and the combined business traded as New Generation McKinley for a couple of years. At this point the company raised its first serious equity round, taking in a little over £800,000 from existing and new shareholders. Most of this was used to pay off debt owed to the original holding company and to reduce the holding of James's original partner.

With the acquisition of McKinley Vintners, New Generation gained several key benefits:

- A strong book of suppliers and customers from a business that had been trading for thirty-five years

- An established presence and reputation in the classic old-world regions, which gave the company access to wines it would not otherwise have been able to get hold of

- A London office which it needed to service a growing business and its suppliers and customers

- An experienced wine-marketing department

Following the acquisition, James and Peter were able to secure replacement agency deals with Champagne Janisson & Fils and ABK6 Cognac to replace the lost contracts. It was the combination of Peter's reputation and track record together with James and his team's ability to execute on the sales side that enabled them to land these contracts, which neither firm on its own would have been able to do.

Today James owns a little more than a third of the business. This is less than the original 50% he started out with, but it is a classic example of owning a smaller stake in a much bigger business. The dilution from one-half to one-third must be considered in the context of the value of that investment.

His acquisition in 2005 was of a company with less than £100,000 in revenues and an operating loss of £70,000. It can't have been worth very much. Over the past fourteen years, James has grown the company's revenues to north of £6 million and EBITDA in excess of £400,000. Looking at deals in the wine trade, growing businesses can be valued in a range from eight to twelve times EBITDA, which means the company could be worth £3.2–4.8 million. James's holding has grown in value from half of not much to a third of £3.2–4.8 million, which is £1.1–1.6 million. That is a clear demonstration of the benefits of growth by acquisition to the founder of a business, despite the dilution of his holding in percentage terms.

James is comfortable that he and his partners can scale the company as it stands to £10 million and beyond. As he puts it, 'We have structured the business as a quality focused, highly relevant wine, champagne and spirits agency business, with a strong emphasis on personal relationships that treat both customers and suppliers as equally important.' And he is not averse to other strategic acquisitions.

Conclusion
It's Time To FACE Your Future

This is where the rubber meets the road. The question now is: how do you FACE Your Future and make it happen?

In the 17th century, the father of modern physics, Sir Isaac Newton, rocked the world with some of his findings – not just the apple falling on his head and 'discovering' gravity, which of course had always existed. Newton was just the first person to provide a scientific explanation, which led to his law of gravity.

Of much greater impact were his three laws of motion, which broadly speaking are:

1. An object will remain at rest or in motion until it is acted on by an outside force

2. The force required to change motion is dependent on the mass and acceleration of the object

3. For every action there is an equal and opposite reaction

What does that have to do with you implementing the FACE methodology? Everything. The first law means that if you want to make a change, you must act. If not, you will either remain at rest (ie go nowhere) or you'll continue what you are currently doing. I'm sure you didn't read this book to do nothing.

The second law means that to act you must exert some force, and that the amount of force you exert depends on the mass and acceleration of the thing you want to change. How big is the business? Is it moving, and if so how quickly?

The third law means you'll face resistance. It won't be easy and there will be challenges along the way, but these laws prove that you can do it. Apply the right force and the business will change. FACE is that force. Let's look at the steps you need to take.

Your internal team

You can't do it alone. Chapter 1 set out the core functions of a business, and you need to have leaders of your sales and marketing, operations and finance teams in place before you start. You have seen how we continued building the team at Huveaux as the business grew, and you must be ready to do the same.

Take your time building the team and be ready to let it evolve as the business grows and changes. Be sure you've got people with the right experience. If you're not sure, there are plenty of good human resources specialists who can help you. Don't be afraid of paying for the right talent. You get what you pay for, and I'm sure you don't want to skimp a few thousand pounds in salary costs that could scupper a deal which could be worth hundreds of thousands or even millions of pounds down the line. If you've taken the FACE methodology seriously, then you'll know you can afford it because these people will be paid for out of the money you raise.

To round things out, I strongly recommend that you hire a personal assistant (PA). It's funny because I remember back in the nineties there was a growing trend to get rid of PAs as a cost saving measure, and it's a mindset that still exists in many businesses today. It's seen as a 'tough leader' thing in the modern economy – I'll admit it, I was one of them myself. The attitude was: 'I don't need a PA. With technology and the internet I can do it all myself'. True, and with the benefit of hindsight, I can see it is one of the stupidest trends in business.

A good PA is worth their weight in gold. Mine certainly is. When you implement the FACE methodology, you're going to have more to do than ever before. Your PA will become your guardian, your gatekeeper and the person who keeps your life under control.

Build this team and nurture them. This is the team who will help you to realise your dreams. You might even offer them the opportunity to buy into the company. Think back to James Booth and the New Generation case study. He offered his key team members the chance to buy in and they've stuck with him throughout the journey.

And remember that your role has now changed. Let your team do their jobs and you focus on yours: finding investors and raising funds; finding attractive companies and acquiring them; working with your team to consolidate the new businesses; and keeping the exit in mind, even if you're not in a hurry. This is the time for you to FACE Your Future.

Your external team

You'll also need good external advisors, particularly your accountants and lawyers. If you're currently dealing with small, local firms, you may need to make a change. They may have been fine when you were a small, local business too, but your ambitions have changed.

Speak with the most senior person in each firm and ask them about their experience with raising external money through debt or equity, and with buying or selling businesses. If they don't fill you with confidence, it's time to start looking for other more experienced advisors.

With that, you have the core people in place who will help you FACE Your Future. Now it's down to you.

The buck stops with you

Apart from running out of money, which you're not going to do now, the only other reason a business fails is because the owner gives up on it. This is where you need to go deep within yourself and test your resolve, which is why I spent time in Part I of the book talking about your business and your head. Because now it's down to you.

Perhaps you've heard the story of US President Harry S Truman and the sign he had on his desk in the Oval Office: 'The buck stops here'. Truman put it there because at the time there was a perception in US government circles that people were avoiding the tough decisions and not taking responsibility. In other words, they were passing the buck. With that sign, he made it clear that he would make the decisions and accept the responsibility. As commander in chief, he had to. In your role in the business you are running, you are that person and the buck has to stop with you.

Are you committed to making it happen? You can FACE Your Future and achieve the financial rewards that will allow you to do everything you ever wanted. There's just one more thing that I ask of you: don't give up. There's no question it will be hard. There will be days when you will think it's all too much and you can't take it anymore. That's when you need to think beyond yourself and draw on others around you.

Your journey is also likely to end up being different to the one you envisioned. Keep your mind on the end goal, and you'll be able to adapt to the changes in course that life will throw at you. The challenges, obstacles and difficulties that you could never have possibly imagined. Keep moving forward. Some days you won't know which direction forward is. If that's the case, give it your best shot. Just keep moving – you can always correct your course when things become clearer.

Let me end this conclusion with another of my favourite quotes:

'It is not the critic who counts; not the man who points out how the strong man stumbles, or where the doer of deeds could have done them better. The credit belongs to the man who is actually in the arena, whose face is marred by dust and sweat and blood; who strives valiantly; who errs, who comes short again and again, because there is no effort without error and shortcoming; but who does actually strive to do the deeds; who knows great enthusiasms, the great devotions; who spends himself in a worthy cause; who at the best knows in the end the triumph of high achievement, and who at the worst, if he fails, at least fails while daring greatly, so that his place shall never be with those cold and timid souls who neither know victory nor defeat.'
— Theodore Roosevelt

Good luck. Enjoy the ride and let me know how you get on. You can reach me by email on dbh@ addthenmultiply.com or on Twitter @David_B_Horne.

APPENDICES

APPENDICES

Appendix 1
EIS And SEIS

If you have an SME business based in the UK, there are two government schemes I'd like to draw your attention to: the Enterprise Investment Scheme (EIS) and the Seed Enterprise Investment Scheme (SEIS). To the best of my knowledge, these schemes are unique to the UK and they make the entire investment proposition much easier by offering attractive tax incentives to investors in qualifying shares. They de-risk the investment proposition, as investors are rightly concerned about the level of risk associated with investments in private companies.

There is uncertainty in less established businesses: their trajectory isn't as predictable, they have less access to resources and are more susceptible to changes in the financial climate. And yet, they can achieve great things given the right opportunity. For this reason, the UK government introduced these attractive tax schemes. They are totally legitimate means for the company to attract investors and increase the likelihood of raising money.

We'll start with EIS, launched in 1993. Under this scheme, you can raise up to £5 million a year and a total of £12 million in the company's lifetime. These amounts are inclusive of other forms of investment, so if you have already raised £2 million in the current financial year, separate to this scheme, you will only be able to raise £3 million under EIS until the end of the year.

How does it work? EIS offers attractive, legitimate tax breaks and credits to investors who are individual UK taxpayers. Any investor paying into an EIS company will get 30% of their initial investment back as a tax credit. So, if an investor puts £1,000 into a company, they can apply to get £300 back. This means that although their investment is worth £1,000 it has only cost them £700.

Not only this, but if the company does well and the shares double in price from £1,000 to £2,000, the investor doesn't have to pay capital gains tax if they decide to sell their shares, so from their investment of £700, they will have made a gain of £1,300 (£2,000 new value of the shares minus £700 initial investment) upon which they don't pay any tax. If the value of the shares stays the same and they sell at £1,000, they have still made a gain of £300 (as they got 30% of their initial investment back) which they don't pay tax on either.

As well as this, if the shares devalue to £700, the investor hasn't made a loss as this was how much they spent in the first place. Finally, if the company goes bust and the shares lose their value, the investor can deduct this loss from their gross income in the year and save on their personal tax bill.

To qualify for both EIS and SEIS, companies must be established in the UK and must not trade on any stock exchange. Technically, AIM is not a stock exchange but an exchange regulated market, which means AIM-listed companies can raise money under EIS if they meet the criteria.

For EIS, the company must also meet these requirements:

- The business needs to have been trading for at least four months, but be under ten years old. That being said, the first commercial sale must have occurred fewer than seven years ago.

- The business must have no more than £15 million in gross assets.

- The business should have fewer than 250 employees.

- Most trades qualify for the scheme, but there are a number of exceptions: banking, financial services, property, leasing, legal and accounting firms, farming, hotels, nursing homes, energy and shipbuilding.

It is vital for small companies to lower the risk of investing so they can attract investors and raise the money they need. A 2014 government report indicated that since EIS was introduced, over 21,000 companies have received investment through the scheme and over £10.7 billion of funds have been raised.

SEIS, introduced in 2012, is similar to EIS, but for much smaller companies. SEIS dramatically reduces the risk of investment. Under this scheme, a company can raise up to £150,000. It works in the same way as EIS, but with even better tax credits: investors who pay into SEIS companies get 50% of their investment back. Using the same example as above, if an investor puts £1,000 into a company, they can apply to get £500 back. This means that although their investment is worth £1,000, it has only cost them £500.

To qualify for SEIS, the company:

- Must be a new business that has been operating for fewer than two years

- Must have no more than £200,000 in gross assets

- Must have fewer than twenty-five employees

Again, most trades qualify for the scheme, and the same business activities as listed under EIS are excluded. But the government is taking a firmer line on the types of companies that do and don't qualify, so it is important that you get professional advice on this.

I have helped several companies to gain approval under HMRC's advance assurance process, so they can approach investors knowing that the investment qualifies.

According to the same 2014 government report as I mentioned earlier, since SEIS was launched, over 1,100 companies have received investment and over £80 million of funds have been raised.

Finally, there are ongoing requirements and restrictions that companies must comply with or the investors will lose their EIS/SEIS relief. Your advisors can inform you of these so you ensure compliance.

It is important to make the most of these schemes as their success has been huge, making the UK the leader in de-risking investments.

Appendix 2
Structures In VC/PE Deals

In most cases, when you are raising equity capital, you'll do it by issuing common or ordinary shares in the company; the terms may differ based on where you are, but these are the normal shares that give the owner a stake in the business. When you raise money through crowdfunding, angel investors and public markets, you'll typically be issuing ordinary shares. When you're raising from VC or PE firms, in the majority of cases, they will add in funding through debt or preference shares.

Let's use an example to illustrate this. Let's say you're doing an MBO and you need to raise £10 million to complete the deal. In cases like this, you will form a new company as the acquisition vehicle. The company will issue a small amount of ordinary shares to you, your team and the PE house. Let's say the split is 55% to you, 5% to your team and 40% to the PE house. The shares will be issued for say £1, so on day one there is £100 of share capital.

Next, the company will issue preference shares to the PE house. These shares might or might not have voting rights, but what they will have is a guaranteed 'dividend' that accrues to the holders of the preference shares. Let's say that the company issues £10 million of preference shares and they include a cumulative dividend of 10% per annum. This means that every year, the holders of these shares accrue £1 million worth of 'dividend'.

I use 'dividend' in quotation marks because under UK and international accounting standards, dividends on preference shares are accounted for like interest expense. If the dividends are cumulative, they happen every year and must be accounted for even if they are not paid out. This serves two purposes:

- It ensures the preference shareholders get a guaranteed return on their investment

- It often wipes out any profit in the business because the £1 million dividend is accounted for like interest expense, so it reduces the company's profits

The new company now has £10,000,100 in cash on its balance sheet, this being the £100 paid in for ordinary shares and the £10 million for preference shares. It then buys the shares in the target company from the former owners. Now you and your management team, together with the PE house, own that business. That's how the MBO works.

Now let's fast forward five years and look at three possible outcomes:

1. Things have gone really well and you sell the company to a trade buyer for £22 million.

2. Things have gone OK and you sell the company for £16 million.

3. Things haven't gone so well and you sell the company for £12 million. It's still a gain on the original £10 million, but as you'll see, it's not a great outcome for you and your team.

What happens is the trade buyer acquires the shares, and typically the acquisition vehicle will be wound up, but it's important to understand the way the money gets paid out.

Starting with outcome 1, you've sold the business to a trade buyer for £22 million, everybody wins. Here's how the cash gets paid out:

• The first £5 million goes to the holders of the preference shares, being the cumulative £1 million dividend every year for five years. For the sake of illustration, I've ignored any impact of compound interest over the years of the dividends not being paid out. This would increase the amount paid here.

- The next £10 million also goes to the holders of the preference shares, being the capital that they paid in for the shares. This gets paid in preference to all other shareholders, hence the name.

- The remaining £7 million goes to the holders of the ordinary shares. Assuming there has been no change to the original allocations, you would get 55% or £3.85 million, your management team would get 5% or £350,000 and the PE firm would get the remaining £2.8 million.

In outcome 2, the cash proceeds of £16 million would be paid out as follows:

- No change on the first £5 million, it's the cumulative dividend.

- No change on the next £10 million, it's the preference shares themselves.

- That leaves £1 million remaining from the proceeds, and again it gets split based on the percentage of ordinary shares. You will get £550,000, your management team £50,000 and the PE house £400,000. Not so attractive, is it? Five years of hard work, and you and the MBO team take 600 grand.

Outcome 3 is even worse for the MBO team. The cash proceeds of £12 million go as follows:

- No change on the first £5 million, it's the cumulative dividend.

- The holders of the preference shares will get the remaining £7 million in settlement for their shares. It's a loss of £3 million compared with what they put in, but at least they get back something.

- The holders of ordinary shares get nothing.

If debt had been put into the business instead of preference shares, it would be broadly the same outcome. The debt would have been secured over the trade and assets of the company, so it gets paid ahead of everything else. There is an order to these things when a company is being wound up: secured creditors are at the front of the queue, followed by unsecured creditors, followed by preference shareholders, and when everyone else has been paid out in full, whatever is left goes to the holders of ordinary shares.

Some people might say that's not fair, but that's the reality of how these deals work. The upside is great for everybody, but the impact of the downside can be serious and the management team can end up with nothing.

Appendix 3
Valuation

I am often asked, 'What is my business worth? How do you value a business?' In reality, it is both an art and a science. The science part is that there are several tried and tested methods for determining the value of a company, while the art part is the selection of one of those methods and the application of all relevant information to determine the value.

In reality, it's an estimation based on information available each day, even for companies listed on a stock exchange, where the share price is updated in real time all day when the market is open. It's still based on the information that is known at the time, and the sentiment of people in the market (which is why share prices often overreact to significant announcements of both good and bad news). As such, it is a highly subjective exercise which requires the valuer to look at historic facts and make assumptions about what might happen in the future.

In the run-up to a general election, the pollsters are continually making predictions about who is going to win or lose, by how much and on and on. It's not until Election Day is over and the ballots have been counted that the real results are known, and it's the same with valuing a business. It's not dissimilar to buying a house. The seller or estate agent will say what the price is, but until the buyer and seller agree the price in an arm's length transaction, it's just someone's best estimate of the value.

Let's explore the science a little bit closer. The most common methods of valuing a business are:

- Capitalisation of earnings, often referred to as the price to earnings (p/e) ratio
- Discounted future cash flow
- Valuing the assets in use
- Entry cost

Under the capitalisation of earnings method, the value is based on the earnings of a business multiplied by a number. For example, let's say a business generated £500K of pre-tax profit and a multiplier (the p/e ratio) of five times was used. This would value the business at £2.5 million (£500K × 5).

Under this method, there are two ways that you can increase the value of the business: either increase profits or increase the multiplier. How do you do that? You know enough about the business to know what to do to increase profits, that's not my responsibility, but I can certainly guide you on how to push for a higher earnings multiplier.

It's not uncommon for small, privately held businesses to sell for multipliers of between three and seven times, and a multiplier of five times is pretty standard. It's also kind of lazy, in my opinion. The way you increase the multiplier is to make your business more attractive as something that will continue to run and grow, without you being involved.

For the PR and marketing services deals that I've done, the multiplier was often based on a matrix that looked at revenue growth and profitability margins. The higher the growth and profit margin, the higher the multiplier. It's not rocket science.

The other key route to increasing the multiplier is to create assets within the business that make it more attractive to a buyer. Is all of your intellectual property (IP) properly registered and protected? Some IP can only be protected for a number of years, and if the time lapses without the protection being renewed then it's open season for a competitor to step in and use the IP you worked hard to develop.

Look at what happened to British Telecom, which developed SMS as a way for its engineers to communicate with each other in the field. It protected this, and then the protection ran out. Imagine if BT earned a royalty from every text message that gets sent today.

Have you documented your systems and processes so that anyone can come into the company and figure out how things get done? Have you got proper contracts in place with staff, customers and suppliers? Things that many entrepreneurs consider boring details can have a huge impact on the value of the company. You'll know how hard it is to increase profits from, say, £500K to £600K. Think instead about the impact that some of these 'boring details' can have on increasing the multiplier from five to seven times instead.

What about things that impact on and reflect company culture, like a certification from Investors in People or an award for being one of the best places to work? Perhaps you've won awards in your industry or local community. Those are assets because they show external validation of what the company has achieved.

Of course, the industry you are in will also have an impact. Steady, stable industries that don't grow much tend to have lower multipliers, while hot industries like FinTech or nanoscience can easily get quite racy multipliers in the double digits.

I remember the heady days of the dotcom boom when people were valuing companies based on measures like sticky eyeballs, ie how long people were visiting the website, or multiples of revenue because the company had yet to turn a profit. From time to time, that still happens in hot sectors like cryptocurrency, but it's only for a select few businesses that happen to be in the right place at the right time. Unicorns don't happen every day.

For companies listed on a stock exchange, you can get all sorts of data from the exchange website that show the p/e ratio based on historic earnings, and if you're willing to do a little more hard work, you can get forward-looking estimates from analysts who are predicting the future results of most listed companies. It's harder for private businesses, although the accounting firm BDO publishes a quarterly *Private Company Price Index* that gives the blended multiple of all private company transactions it was able to find. In 2018 it captured and reported on over 2,500 deals and came up with an average multiplier of 10.4, although it included an important caveat in that number: reported profits of privately held owner-managed companies can be depressed by non-recurring or non-business expenses that the owners put through the books.

Discounted cash flow (DCF) is the method preferred by Warren Buffett when he values a business. Buffett looks closely at the historic cash flows of the companies he is interested in, and based on their historic performance, he projects cash flows into the future. Remember that Buffett's approach is never to sell companies; he describes his ideal holding period as forever. Therefore he forecasts the cash a long way into the future using different financial models. He then takes that future cash flow and works out what it is worth in terms of money today, using a financial formula called net present value. This method is best used with more established companies that have a track record over a number of years. It's hard to use DCF on young companies because there is no baseline of historical performance to build from.

When you're looking at asset-based valuation, look at both gross assets and net assets. Gross assets is all of the assets that are in the company, as presented on the balance sheet in its published financial statements. Net assets is gross assets less liabilities, which is equal to shareholders' equity, again as presented on the balance sheet.

The downside of using this method is that accounting standards were not developed with valuation in mind. For example, things like fixed assets, which are used in the business over many years, are accounted for at their original costs and then written down by depreciation. So it might be that you have built some really cool tech over the last three years that is driving the business, but under the accounting rules, much of that cost has been charged to depreciation and the carrying value of the asset is nothing near to its revenue-generation capabilities today.

Finally, entry cost looks at valuation in the context of what it would cost to set up a directly competing business in the same market. This is a simple method of valuation, but to my mind it's rather unsophisticated. It's one thing to work out how much it costs to set up a website, kit out an office, hire ten people and buy some stock and fixed assets. It's another thing entirely to put a value on the industry knowledge a company gains, the contacts it makes with customers and suppliers, the development of the way things get done. Those intangibles are hard to quantify.

As a fan of Warren Buffett, I would always opt for the DCF method where the information is available. With many entrepreneur-led companies, that's just not the case, and the fallback position is to use the capitalisation of earnings method.

Appendix 4
Shareholders' Agreement

In privately held companies with multiple shareholders, it is common to have a shareholders' agreement. This is a legal document between each of the shareholders and the company. It's important that the company is a party to the agreement, as in the event of any disputes under the deal, the company is the overarching entity and has the obligation to ensure the agreement is upheld.

In company law, the first place to look at things that affect the shareholders is the articles of association, but in the UK, this is a document that is in the public domain, and there may be aspects of things between the shareholders that you wish to keep private. These are addressed in the shareholders' agreement.

The shareholders' agreement is the rulebook for how the company is run. No two agreements will be the same, but as with most legal documents, there is a generally accepted framework:

- Who are the directors? Directors of a company have statutory duties to the company and many powers. It is important that all shareholders know the identity of the directors and what roles they play in the business, for example CEO, CFO, etc.

- Who has the right to appoint directors? In many agreements, shareholders who own more than a stated percentage of the company (often 10% or more) will have the right to appoint a director to represent their interests. The director may be the shareholder themselves, but it doesn't have to be.

- What are the rules for board meetings and shareholder meetings? There will be a schedule of formal meetings for both the board and the shareholders, and the basis for this will be set out in the agreement. For example, the board meets monthly and the shareholders meet annually within ninety days of the end of the financial year.

- What matters require the approval of the directors or the shareholders? In addition to the regularity of meetings, there are often certain matters that are reserved for the approval of the board or the shareholders. Approval might mean a majority in some cases and unanimous in others. For example, approving the budget might require a majority of directors; a major acquisition might require unanimous approval of the directors and a majority of the shareholders.

- What are the rules when a shareholder wants to leave? Ownership of the shares is usually tightly controlled and it is not uncommon to require a shareholder to offer their shares to the other shareholders before an outside person has the opportunity to buy them. Equally, should none of the other shareholders wish to buy, there must be rules that enable a shareholder to sell.

- What are the restrictions on a departing shareholder? They will likely cover confidentiality, non-compete and non-solicit provisions which restrict the departing shareholder from taking action to the detriment of the company and the remaining shareholders.

- What happens when a new shareholder comes in? The standard approach here is to have an appendix to the agreement called a deed of adherence. This is a shorter document that effectively binds in the new shareholder to the existing agreement without having to reissue the entire document.

- What is the dividend policy? Depending on the nature of the business and its investors, some shareholders will want to know if there will be the possibility of dividend payments, and if so how these will be calculated and made.

- What happens in a proposed change of control? Let's say the company is now looking to an exit. There are often provisions in the agreement referred to as drag-along and tag-along. Drag-along provisions enable a majority of shareholders (it could be 75% or it could be certain named shareholders like the founding team) to require the minority holders to follow them in a sale transaction on the same terms as they are selling at. This stops the minority from blocking such a transaction, because the minority is dragged along. Tag-along provisions are the other side of the coin. These ensure that if a majority of shareholders sell, the minority shareholders have the right to participate in the transaction rather than being left behind. They tag along with the majority.

The list can extend from there, but it's really a case of making sure the rules of engagement are known and understood by all parties. As with any of the legal documents and processes referred to in this book, if you are going to put a shareholders' agreement in place, be sure to use a qualified lawyer to do so. It's not expensive. It might cost a few thousand pounds, but if you're following the FACE methodology, that is not something that will hold you back.

Bibliography

Banks, Sydney – (2001) *The Enlightened Gardener*. Vancouver, Canada, Lone Pine Publishing

Covey, Stephen R – (1989) *The 7 Habits of Highly Effective People*. London, UK, Simon & Schuster

Cremades, Alejandro – (2016) *The Art of Startup Fundraising*. Hoboken, USA, John Wiley & Sons

Dooley, Mike – (2010) *Manifesting Change*. New York, USA, Atria Books and Beyond Words

Frankl, Viktor – (2004) *Man's Search for Meaning*. London, UK, Rider, an imprint of Ebury Publishing

Gates, Bill – (1995) *The Road Ahead*. London, UK, Viking Publishing

Hagstrom, Robert G – (1999) *The Warren Buffett Portfolio*. New York, USA, John Wiley & Sons

Isaacson, Walter – (2011) *Steve Jobs: The Exclusive Biography*. London, UK, Little Brown Book Group

Meldrum, Mike and McDonald, Malcolm – (2000) *Marketing in Manageable Bites*. London, UK, Macmillan Press

Neill, Michael – (2013) *The Inside Out Revolution*. London, UK, Hay House

Neill, Michael – (2018) *Creating the Impossible*. London, UK, Hay House

Priestley, Daniel – (2018) *Entrepreneur Revolution*. London, UK, John Wiley & Sons

Priestley, Daniel – (2017) *24 Assets*. London, UK, Rethink Press

Roddick, Anita – (2005) *Business as Unusual*. London, UK, Anita Roddick Books

Sinek, Simon – (2009) *Start with Why*. London, UK, Penguin Books

Wickman, Gino – (2011) *Traction*. Dallas, USA, BenBella Books Inc.

Acknowledgements

There are so many people to thank, it's actually a little daunting because I'd hate to leave anyone out, but invariably that's going to happen. If you're one of them, I'm sorry. My bad.

Starting with my mum, Tricia Horne, who turned ninety this year and whose zest for life is inspiring. It's the best game in town. My late dad, John Horne, who taught me so much about money and business at an early age and always encouraged me to get out there and try things. Thank you.

My wife Kate, whom I met when we were both seventeen. You are my rock, my life partner and my soulmate. Our daughters Vicky and Madsie, who challenge me, support me, tease me, and demonstrate every day what a joy it is to have kids, even when they are grown up. I love you more than you could ever imagine.

Turning to actually writing this book, it has to start with Daniel Priestley and the team at Dent Global – Andrew, Donna, Krizia, Toma and the rest. Completing the Key Person of Influence Accelerator was one of the best things I've done, and I can honestly say that it changed my life.

Tim Sutton and Marty Franken at BSMG Worldwide, where I did my first acquisitions. Angela Heylin, also at BSMG, who introduced me to John van Kuffeler, the man who – more than any other – taught me my craft. Friends and colleagues at Huveaux (in chronological order as best I can remember): John Clarke, Pam Anson, Jean-Marie Simon, Marcelle du Plessis, Emma Mallinson, Ingrid Amiri, Simon Thompson, Alain Trébucq, Catherine Corre, Dan O'Brien and Mike Arnaouti. John Allbrook, Gisa Bielfeldt, Adrian Pang, Bob Scriven and Nick Taylor at GoIndustry-DoveBid, along with my finance team – John Boulton, Andy Fleischer, Elke Rockenhäuser, Andy Shipway and Mark Yu. And Tes Cervania, who left the team but always stayed in touch. Thank you for everything you have taught me.

To all my clients/friends since I started my own business – Navid and Ifti at Alchemiya; Pallab and Rob at Apollo; Julia at Bold Clarity; James, Grant and the team at Central Working: Fabio, Paolo and Stefano at Chupamobile; Daniel and the team at Dent; Nan at Four; Matt at ICPS; Rocco and Jacqui at Landmark Europe; Martin and the team at The Centre; Dhru and the team at Tubules; Jason, James and the team at Welcome Gate; and many more. Thank you for your trust and belief in me.

To business advisors who have become good friends – Delphine Currie, Jamie Mathieson, Mary Monfries, Ronald Paterson.

To James Booth for agreeing to share his story. He has built the kind of business I wanted to when I started in the wine trade, but it wasn't meant to be.

To four brave souls who agreed to be test readers and gave so much useful and constructive feedback on the first draft of this book – Rupa Datta, Sara Halton, Vincent Herlaar and Mark Robinson. Your input has been invaluable, and you have my deepest thanks.

To Michael Neill, Jo Winchcombe, Damian Mark Smyth, Fiona Klat and Helen Oakwater, who have coached me over the last few years. I am grateful for your wisdom, love and guidance.

To the team at Rethink Press – Lucy, Joe, Kate, Anke, and especially Alison whose careful editing helped make the final version of the book so much better.

To Dhru Shah, who gets an extra mention because he is the one who gave me the final kick up the bum to actually write the book I'd been talking about since he saw me at the KPI Pitchfest event in early 2016.

And to everyone else who has made a mark on my life. There are so many, and I thank you all.

The Author

David B Horne was born
and raised on the west coast
of Canada. He qualified as a
Chartered Accountant with
Price Waterhouse (now part
of PwC) in 1987. Later that
year, he and his wife moved
to Zürich, Switzerland where
David continued his career.
Both of their daughters were
born in Zürich.

He left Price Waterhouse in 1989 and joined his largest
client, NCR Switzerland, as financial controller. In
1993, David and his family moved from Zürich to
London, where he continued with NCR. During this

time, AT&T acquired NCR, and in 1995 he transferred to AT&T Capital. In 1997, David joined the BBC in his first finance director role. Three years later, he joined BSMG Worldwide as CFO Europe, where he made his first business acquisitions, buying seven PR agencies in two years.

He launched his consultancy business in 2002 and ran it for a year, before being appointed in 2003 as CFO of Huveaux plc, which was listed on London's Alternative Investment Market (AIM). In three years, he raised over £60 million with Huveaux and bought seven more companies. He left in 2006 to become CFO of GoIndustry plc, which had just listed on AIM. There he raised over £40 million and acquired a global competitor. In 2010, he resigned from GoIndustry.

At the end of 2010, David launched a wine business, Horne & Daughters, serving private clients and investing on Liv-ex, the London International Vintners Exchange. He also re-launched his consulting business, and now works exclusively with entrepreneurs implementing his FACE methodology. Over his career, David has bought or sold more than twenty companies.

A colleague of David's from the BBC describes him as an explorer of people, places and possibilities. He speaks fluent German, reasonable French and basic Italian.

He lives in London with his wife, Kate.